Why Odysseus Came Home

as a Stranger and other

Puzzling Moments in the Life of

BUDDHA, SOCRATES, JESUS, ABRAHAM,

and other Great Individuals

by

HENRY ABRAMOVITCH

CHIRON PUBLICATIONS • ASHEVILLE, NORTH CAROLINA

www.ChironPublications.com

Interior and cover design by Danijela Mijailovic
Printed primarily in the United States of America.

ISBN 978-1-63051-772-4 paperback
ISBN 978-1-63051-773-1 hardcover
ISBN 978-1-63051-774-8 electronic
ISBN 978-1-63051-775-5 limited edition paperback

Library of Congress Cataloging-in-Publication Data

Names: Abramovitch, Henry, 1950- author.
Title: Why Odysseus came home as a stranger and other puzzling moments in the life of Buddha, Socrates, Jesus, Abraham, and other great individuals / Henry Abramovitch.
Description: Asheville : Chiron Publications, 2020. | Includes biblio-graphical references. | Summary: "Author Henry Abramovitch comes from a culture that encourages people to ask why. As a Jungian analyst, he also values questions. In reading the life stories of "Great Individuals," he often found himself asking the question, "Why?" Why did Arjuna, greatest general of his age refuse to fight? Why did Socrates remember his debt to Ascalapius, the god of healing, only in his last breath? Why did Jesus, the prophet of love, curse an innocent fig tree? Why did Odysseus come home as a stranger? The short essays in this book do not try to answer these questions, but they do provide a response, enriched by Jewish tradition and Jungian psychology"-- Provided by publisher.
Identifiers: LCCN 2020016261 (print) | LCCN 2020016262 (ebook) | ISBN 9781630517724 (paperback) | ISBN 9781630517731 (hardcover) | ISBN 9781630517748 (ebook)
Subjects: LCSH: Jungian psychology. | Jewish philosophy.
Classification: LCC BF173.J85 A27 2020 (print) | LCC BF173.J85 (ebook) | DDC 150.19/54--dc23
LC record available at https://lccn.loc.gov/2020016261
LC ebook record available at https://lccn.loc.gov/2020016262

Table of Contents

Preface

I come from a culture that encourages people to ask why. The first ritual performance of a Jewish child is to ask four questions at the Passover seder. Significantly, the child never really receives answers to these questions. It is the questions that count, not the answers. As Rilke wrote: "...try to love the questions themselves, ... Live the questions now..."[1] In the world of Jewish learning, the highest praise is given, not to one knows all the answers, but to the student who comes up with new, creative questions that challenge us to see things in a new way.

As a Jungian analyst, I also value questions. In many ways, the work of analysis is an ever-ongoing pursuit of "Why?" In my work, some of my most effective interventions are not actual interpretations, but questions that open up new ground. In reading the life stories of "Great Individuals," I often found myself asking the question, "Why?" Why did Arjuna, greatest general of his age, refuse to fight? Why did Socrates remember his debt to Asclepius, the god of healing, only in his last breath? Why did Jesus, the prophet of love, curse an innocent fig tree? Why did Abraham agree to kill the son he loved the most? Why did Lot's wife look back? Why did Odysseus come home as a stranger?

The short essays in this book do not try to answer these questions, but they do provide a response, enriched by Jewish tradition and Jungian psychology. They are not trying to prove a point or confirm a theory. Each chapter, however, does touch on broader issues that derive from specific conundrums, such as the process of home-coming, the psychology of the impossible, the impact of trauma upon memory, the need for an end of illness ritual, different types of forgiveness, the relation of aggression to compassion, the psychology of silence, the psychology of the revolutionary, and the dilemma of succession, among other topics.

In my discussions, I draw on my professional expertise as both Jungian analyst and anthropologist. My portrayal of these seminal figures is as living personalities, with very human dilemmas and not as the idealized figures they became. I use traditional sources from within these traditions and accept those texts, uncritically, as a believer sees them. I am certainly not an expert on all these sources. But I have benefited greatly from my friends who are knowledgeable in specific areas: David Shulman, Jonathan Price, George Savran, Jim Ponet, Shlomi Naeh, and Yohanan Grinspoon. I want to thank my daughter Tamara for suggesting Goya's "Dog" for the book cover and my wife Iva for her skillful editing. I want to give special thanks to Murray Stein for his timely encouragement. I sincerely wish to thank the Chiron team for their creative effort in bringing this "why" book into fruition.

Each chapter may be read separately, although some themes interweave among the essays. I have also included some essays, such as "Why do men wear ties?" which, although not discussing a great personality, are written in the same spirit of inquiry.

Henry Abramovitch, Jerusalem

Why Arjuna Refused to Fight

The opening scene of the *Bhagavad Gita*[2] warms the heart of the pacifist in us all. Arjuna, the world's greatest warrior, has assembled a coalition of armies to fight what was to be the very first World War. His cause is just. His evil cousins have stolen the kingdom from him and his brothers. Despite all their gracious attempts at compromise and mediation, Arjuna and his brothers have been shut out, ridiculed and humiliated. There appears to be no other way to regain their rightful place except through force of arms. Both sides have enlisted allies and are about to meet for the decisive clash at the crucial battle near modern Delhi. Everything is ready for battle. Everyone is waiting for Arjuna to give the signal to attack.

Arjuna asks his charioteer, who is no other than Lord Krishna, to drive to the open ground between the two armies. He wants to get a better look at who he is about to fight and kill. Then something unpredicted happens. Looking on the other side, he sees his cousins, his friends, his kinsmen and his teacher. Arjuna's heart melts. His tongue becomes dry, his arms fail, a shudder runs through his whole body. His famous bow, Gandiva, slips from his weakened hand. He becomes feverish and his skin parched. His life within him seems to swim and, becoming faint, he can hardly stand. No wonder the opening section of Gita is called "The Book of the Distress of Arjuna." He turns to Krishna and asks, "How can I shed our common blood?" He goes on to say that nothing good can come from the impending mutual slaughter. Arjuna asks, "Shall I kill these [brothers, fathers-in-law, sons-in-law, elders, and friends] even though they want to kill me?" He continues in this vein: "If they be guilty, we shall grow guilty by their deaths. Their sin will light on us... What peace can come from that?" He considers the chaotic impact of the destruction on their homes, their womenfolk, even their ancestors. Sick at heart, Arjuna drops his weapons and slumps down into his chariot seat. Instead of leading the charge, he refuses to fight.

The *Bhagavad Gita* or "Lord's Song" has been called the single most important text of Hinduism and is a vital synopsis of the religious thought of India. My concern, however, is not with Indian mysticism, but with Arjuna's great refusal, to borrow a term from Dante. He is the first truly conscientious objector. At a crucial moment, he recognizes the essential humanity of his enemies. His passion is not that of some youth, afraid of blood and guts, nor of one wavering in the justice of his cause. This is a *volte-face* of the Field Marshall himself. It is as if General Eisenhower on D-Day had said, "We cannot go in folks. The Germans are just people like ourselves." If Krishna had not forced him back toward his karmic, caste duty, he would surely be the patron saint of war rejectors.

The text presents Arjuna's decision as an impulsive overflow of compassion, surprising, above all to himself. No reason is given. Arjuna's feeling and decision seem so out of character, that one feels compelled to ask: Why does Arjuna refuse to fight?

I believe the roots of this melting of a warrior's iron resolve, lie in a previous, and most peculiar, episode in the life of Arjuna. To understand the impact of this specific episode, we need to broaden the picture. Although the Gita is often sold as a separate volume—I first encountered it in the heyday of the Hare Krishna movement, when it was thrust upon me by chanting bhakti-devotees at an airport—it is actually part of a much greater work, the *Mahabharata*.

The *Mahabharata* is surely one of the longest and most complex works of art ever composed, saying of itself "...what is not found here, is nowhere."[3] The epic deals with so much, but the main plot concerns the five Pandava brothers (named for their common father Pandu), who struggle with their first cousins (the 100 sons of their father's blind brother) for control of their kingdom. Such sibling-like rivalry is as old as Cain and Abel, Seth and Osiris, and Romulus and Remus. What is extraordinary is how the Pandavas' marital destiny creates the opposite: brotherly love.

7

Arjuna, third in birth, but first in battle order, wins a bride, Draupadi, through a traditional archery contest. Coming home, he calls to his mother from outside their abode saying, "We have a gift for you, mother." The mother, thinking the gift was an offering of alms, replies in the spirit of cooperation, "Share it equally with your brothers." In India, a mother's words are sacred. The brothers are, therefore, obliged to share Arjuna's wife. In this unexpected way, Draupadi becomes the common wife of all five brothers. Miraculously, all five brothers come to love Draupadi as the god of love entered the heart of each brother equally. She lived as the wife of each brother in turn in a unique serial monogamy-cum-fraternal polyandry. The brother-husbands introduced a rule: if any brother discovered another in the act of making love to Draupadi, that brother-voyeur would retire to the forest for twelve years of exile, as indeed happened once to Arjuna himself. The Pandavas, in their remarkable ability to share the love for one woman, clearly exemplify the positive pole of the sibling archetype. Here brothers live together, while so many other brothers, trapped in a scarcity psychology of envy and deprivation, would literally or metaphorically be at each other's throats. It is the first occasion in the epic when expected war is turned into unexpected love.

The Pandava brothers continue struggling with their "evil cousins" for control of their kingdom. The Pandavas are portrayed as willing to compromise, while their power-hungry cousins are not. They desire the entire kingdom exclusively for themselves and are unwilling to take turns. Family studies have revealed that disputes between young children about taking turns were more likely to end in tears and very angry outbursts than any disputes between parent and child.[4] The intensity of the conflict is therefore typical of sibling psychology. The uncle-advisor to the cousins realizes that Arjuna's eldest brother, Yudishthera, has a single weakness. He is addicted to games of chance. Hindu culture views any excessive attachments as the ultimate source of suffering. The cousins seductively invite Yudishthera to a game of dice, to which he naively agrees. In the presence of his brothers, Yudishthera proceeds to lose everything. In India, everything literally means every "thing": jewels, palaces, kingdom, brothers, and ultimately, himself. Finally, he is willing to bet all against their wife, Draupadi and, with a loser's luck, he loses her as well. Wife and brothers go off for years of exile.

According to the agreement at the end of the dice game, the five brothers must spend their last year of exile in disguise, "so that even the gods themselves will not recognize them." Coming to the Kingdom of Virata, Arjuna hides their weapons in the tangled branches of a huge tree, hanging a corpse in the branch, hoping the stench will keep curiosity seekers away. When questioned about the corpse by local shepherds, they say that it is their mother's and their custom is to dangle corpses from branches.

Inside the Kingdom of Virata, each brother embraces his shadow identity, claiming to be a close companion of themselves. The shadow is usually the dark instinctual side of the personality that we least want to recognize, as is the case for Dr. Jekyl and Mr. Hyde. But sometimes the shadow may compensate in a positive way and become a "light shadow" containing positive parts, and this is the case for the Pandavas. Yudishtheta takes on the guise of a Brahmin, who teaches the science of dice. Unlike the real Yudishthera, the shadow-Yudishthera succeeds in making his gamblers win every time. Draupadi works as a hairdresser to the queen, serving in the creation of ever-elegant feminine beauty. She does for the queen what was done for her when she was in the royal chair. Bima, the strongman with an ever-enormous appetite, becomes a cook, the prince of pots. It is one of the best examples of sublime-making, transforming taking into giving. Arjuna's change is the most dramatic. Arjuna, appears as a woman, wearing jewelry, earrings, gold bangles, and long hair.

The Sanskrit text of the *Mahabharata* employs a creative ambiguity concerning Arjuna's gender status. It is not clear whether the new dancing master is a woman, a eunuch, a transvestite, or a true transsexual with vagina and breasts. It is not unlikely that he was a "third sex" neither male nor female, and who are now given official standing throughout the Indian subcontinent. The only thing that is certain is that he is no longer a man—let alone that most masculine of warriors.

The king orders an examination and the women confirm that Arjuna, now called Brihannala, has what it takes to be declared female. He, or now she, is hired as the dancing master for the princess and palace ladies of the king's harem. Arjuna—Brihannala—spends the year dancing in the king's harem. During that year of disguise, Arjuna as Brihannala enters deeply into the secret experience of the feminine. Most men encounter their feminine through the projection of an idealized "anima" onto a specific love. When the beloved does not fit his ideal, the gap between the outer and inner feminine is revealed. Such experiences help a man to discover his inner feminine, which Jung called anima, using the Latin word for soul. Alternatively, men encounter the feminine side in dreams, fantasy, and products of the imagination. For example, a man may dream of an alluring unknown woman, an image of his unknown anima. Arjuna's experience suggests that there is a third, more radical way of knowing the feminine: by "becoming a woman" in the imaginative space that an epic makes possible.

The ability to become another gender has always intrigued human imagination.[5] Arjuna's transgender experience is not only the stuff of epics, but is found in many unexpected places. The Bible explicitly forbids cross-dressing, clearly showing that such practices were well known, even in ancient times.[6] Many Native American cultures included the special social category of "Berdache," a man who dressed and lived as a woman. The Berdache were especially widespread among the

11

Plains Indians. According to one account, they were permitted to sing but not dance. They would go to war, though not with a bow and arrow, only with a club, very much as Arjuna does. They attended the band council and nothing would be decided without their advice. As sacred "twin-spirits," they held together the opposites of feminine and masculine, and as a result, possessed special wisdom.

More dramatic varieties of transgender experience are found in many other cultures and are a distinct aspect of the society. Indian males, sometimes called Hijras,[7] may castrate themselves to honor their Goddess, reminiscent of a similar cult of Cybele in the ancient world. The Mahu of Hawaii includes a wide semantic field of intersexuality that has no English equivalent: women who dress and work as men, men who dress and work as women, women or men who dress to conceal their biological classification, women who only associate with other women, men who dress "festively," those whom Westerners call "gay," men who undergo hormonal or surgical procedures, and true hermaphrodites. Mahu of all sorts are highly sought to provide childcare since they are considered particularly compassionate and creative.[8]

We tend to think of animals as either male or female, but within the animal kingdom, there are remarkable exceptions that are both. Some plants and animals are hermaphrodite (the word itself combines Greek gods, Hermes and Aphrodite). But even more exceptional, are fish who are "sequential hermaphrodites," and which regularly undergo "gender switching."[9] In some species, it is a normal part of the life cycle. These fish begin life as males and progress to being females in the second half of life; other species are context-sensitive: when the female gender is scarce, a male fish may become female, at least until other females arrive, whereupon it may switch back to its original masculine identity, much as Arjuna does.

Arjuna's male-to-female-to-male transformation recalls the experience of Tiresias in Greek mythology. Tiresias, as a young man, saw two snakes copulating and for some reason threw a rock at them. For this act, he was instantly turned into a woman. Tiresias lived as a woman, until once again he happened upon snakes in the act of mating. Hoping for a repetition transformation, he stoned this mating pair and was magically transformed back into a man. Like Arjuna, Tiresias had a unique experience of life in both gender modes. A quarrel in Olympus drew on his unique expertise. Hera and Zeus were having one of their many domestic quarrels about Zeus' notorious infidelities. They argued about who derives greater pleasure from the act of making love, the man or the woman. Each claimed that the other gender had the greater part of pleasure. To settle the matter empirically, they called upon Tiresias to testify. To Hera's dismay, Tiresias said that women have ninety percent of the sexual pleasure, while men had barely the remaining ten percent. Enraged at his evidence, Hera blinded him;

Zeus consoled Tiresias by giving him second sight. Tiresias became a famous blind prophet, who could see secrets from the past and into the future. Tiresias revealed to Oedipus the truth about his past, namely, how Oedipus had married his mother and murdered his father, Laius. It was Tiresias who had said that Narcissus would live long, but only if only he will not know himself. In the Underworld, as told in the Odyssey, Tiresias told Odysseus what he must do to finally come home in peace, as will be discussed in the chapter on Odysseus.

The transgender experiences of Tiresias and Arjuna were, until very recently, things of fantasy, fairytale, or psychosis. One of Freud's most famous cases histories concerns a German High Court Judge, Daniel Schreiber, who had undergone a severe psychotic episode in which he had believed he was turning into a woman. In a period of sanity, he wrote a remarkable account of this journey through madness. It was later discovered that his father was a sex-obsessed sadist, brutal even by perverse Prussian standards—he advocated placing babies in ice cube baths and children into metal corsets. No wonder Schreiber the son felt he was undergoing "soul murder," who had consented to becoming a "woman," and who had to submit as a matter of survival.[10]

In many respects, Arjuna's experience, a man living as a woman, resembled a "real life test." This test requires that individuals transitioning out of their birth gender must live as the opposite sex in order to qualify for sexual reassignment surgery. People who feel trapped in the wrong body can become the sex they want to be, but it is important that they are sure. Since unlike Arjuna or Teiresias, once a man is surgically feminized, or a woman masculinized, there is no going back in that way.

However, a recent case report[11] presented the surprising case of a successful switch in another way. A man had been married and fathered three children. He divorced and married another woman, but after a year of marriage announced that he did indeed want to spend the rest of his life with his wife, but as her wife. He successfully assumed the female role. A number of years later, his wife, as part of her seminary training was assigned to a fundamentalist church. This church, it was known, would never accept a lesbian pastor, married to a transgendered individual. Out of love and loyalty, he offered to resume male dress for the duration of her internship, to support and protect her partner. He would temporarily return to his male persona for family gatherings and to council his wayward son. The temporary switch back to an outward male persona, made him feel like a woman masquerading as a man and truly consolidated his female identity. This case of male to female to male and back to female goes one step beyond Arjuna's experience.

Returning to our question: Why did Arjuna refuse to fight? War is the masculine profession, par excellence. The male gods of war, whether Mars or Thor, embody masculine values. To be a warrior means to

15

suppress the feminine qualities of compassion and caring. To be a warrior means to harden one's heart as much as one's muscles; to cut oneself off emotionally from the human consequences of the impending human catastrophe. As General Patton said, "I don't want you to die for your country. I want the other guy to die for his country."[12] To be a soldier is above all "to be a man." In so many societies, the culturally approved way in which one enacts one's masculinity and proves oneself to be a "real man" is bravery in battle. For most soldiers and their macho imitators, the "feminine" represents a profound threat to their fighting identity. This fear is often expressed symbolically by forbidding any literal or symbolic contact between soldiers and women before battle. Women are prohibited from touching a man's arms in both senses of the word "arms." Feminine parts of the psyche are suppressed and denied. The traditional and ritual humiliation of untested recruits often uses an archetypal insult: "You are just a bunch of old women!" They, like Schreiber, become terrified of turning into "women" who are weak and vulnerable.

Arjuna's identity as a soldier derives from his birth identity as a member of the caste of warriors. It is hard for a choice-ridden modern to understand the psychological imperative that caste conveys. For Arjuna, fighting is not a matter of choice; it is a matter of destiny, a way of carrying out Divine wishes. But Arjuna had one formative experience that no other field general ever had. He knew what it was like to be a woman, from the inside.

Imagine what it was like for this great soldier to hang up his weapons and concentrate on rhythm and dance. I believe that during this year in Virata, Arjuna experienced the feminine that is repressed in every warrior. Jung taught that if you are overly identified with one part of the personality, then the psyche will provide a corrective compensation. The less one pays attention, the more forceful the message will become in nightmares, phobias, or bad luck. Arjuna's persona was certainly over-identified with his social role as the masculine, heroic warrior. He was either a hero or nothing else. The Virata year turned him inside out. His feminine came out, so he discovered an aspect of the human experience that he would never otherwise have known. Hinduism teaches that the *atman* is beyond gender, and Jung believed that about the Self as well. We are all born into a fixed caste-like gender identity that clearly determines identity. Yet there is a part of ourselves that transcends the experience of who we are. In the freedom of that imagination space we can enter deeply into who we are not and a man can certainly become a woman, like Arjuna did.

There are specific differences between women and men. But from a psychological perspective one of the most robust distinctions between masculine and feminine modes lies along the instrumental-affective divide. Traditionally, men, or rather the masculine, like to get things done. Women, or rather the feminine, care about how things get done, about feelings and relationships. Women everywhere provide the emotional glue, holding families together. This concern has nothing to do with anatomy, since there are plenty of men who function well in the caring mode, and certainly lots of go-getting women.

The warrior role is based upon the suppression of feminine sensibilities in favor of getting the job done. In the words of a famous football coach, "Winning isn't the most important thing, it is the only thing!"[13] This motto may be only symbolically true in sports, but it is dangerously true in warfare. Masculine fighters want to win. They want to be able to hold their head high. They certainly do not want to talk about how it feels to lose. That is for sissies, men who are overly feminine.

Young men often define their masculine identity in opposition to women. In some cultures, the fear of turning into a woman is explicit and must be overcome by vigorous efforts. Not being masculine enough is equated with being feminine and so warriors fear the feminine. When challenged, the masculine "warrior" must respond. He must fight or lose face. To back down undermines a man's sense of his own masculinity. Cowardice, or even caution, is identified with the feminine and despised. An insecure man will always fear being called "a woman." A "macho" man always needs to prove and re-prove his hyper-masculinity. A macho man (who is by definition always insecure about his masculinity and uninitiated into a more mature kind of manhood) would rather die than be called feminine. That

is why unmanning questions, such as, "Are you calling
me a coward?" so often lead to such violent attempts to
prove the accusation false.

The feminine mode allows for choices. A person
operating in this non-masculine way can decide to fight
or not fight. She may back down and withdraw because
she does not want to injure the relationship. It is the same
logic that allows women to be victimized by masculine
power tactics. But a woman does not have to prove that
she is a "man," and she can never prove she is a "woman"
by fighting back.

Arjuna, looking over the lines of battle, saw them
suddenly through the eyes of Brihannala. He saw the
feminine consequences of battle and the family tragedy
that would mean the victors would also lose. As a man,
Arjuna would fight literally at all costs; but having been
a woman, he knew he could not. In Hebrew, the word for
compassion, *rachamin,* is the plural of the word for
womb, *rechem.* Compassion is the voice of the collective
feminine speaking from their ability to become mothers.
Like a true pacifist, he felt it was better to die than to kill.
One can almost hear the Brinhannala in Arjuna say,
"Make dance, not war!"

During the ensuing war, there is another moment
when Arjuna is consumed by compassion. It occurs
when he is fighting his half-brother and great rival,
Karna. Karna was born to their mother Kunti before she
married Arjuna's father Pandu. Unable to raise her son
as a single mother, Kunti set the baby afloat on a river,

like the mother of Moses and the mother of the great
Mesopotamian king, Sargon the Great. Karna was found
and raised by a low-caste couple. Karna, like many
heroes, has two sets of parents, his actual simple one and
his secret, royal ones, which Jung understood as the
universal, inner tension between personal parents who
care for you and archetypal parents who reveal your
destiny. Karna's life is saturated by this tension. He came
to the kingdom and was invited to join the side of the
cousins, not knowing his true identity as Arjuna's eldest
brother. His mother revealed his birth identity and
unconscious kinship to the Pandavas only on the eve of
the great battle. Kunti begged him to switch sides to
become rightful king of the Pandava. Karna is faced with
a dilemma between his birth karma and his dharma. He
must choose between his birth brothers and his adopted
brothers, between who he is now and who he was
supposed to be. Karna rejects Kunti as the archetypal
mother of destiny and elects to stay with those who have
been loyal to him.

During the height of the battle, these two
brothers, Karna and Arjuna, square off, in an epic within
the epic. At one point in the fighting, Karna's chariot
becomes stuck in the mud and he must change the wheel.
Arjuna holds off, as compassion, brotherhood, and rules
of war require. Arjuna's charioteer, Krishna, an avatar of
the Divine Vishnu, urges Arjuna to press his advantage
and to murder his helpless brother-warrior. Arjuna
hesitates. Karna, weak and vulnerable is at his most

feminine. Arjuna knows that killing a man when he is down is wrong. The story of Arjuna raises ultimate concerns that have no clear answer: When is winning the only thing? And when is doing the right thing, the only thing—even when it leads to catastrophe? When must compassion rule and when unremitting aggression? Arjuna's agony is to decide when not to fight, when he should, and when to fight, when he should not. Or in more symbolic terms, when to dance and when to kill? When to be masculine and when to be feminine? Because each one of us has the potential to be fully both feminine and masculine, the epic calls us to join Arjuna in his hesitations and dwell in that ethical space. Ultimately, Arjuna does kill Karna, his helpless brother and attains victory. But his victory is tainted, as victory always is.

Why Odysseus Came Home Dressed Like a Stranger

The *Odyssey* is one of the most thrilling stories ever composed.[14] The very word for a journey of daring and endurance is embodied in its name, an odyssey. Memorable episodes have left their imprint on the European cultures and languages and within the human psyche: sirens, the Trojan horse, lotus eaters, caught between Scylla and Charybdis, rosy fingers of dawn, descent to the underworld, and more.

Homecoming and its difficulties are the unifying themes of Homer's epic. In the first half of the epic, Odysseus has all of his memorable adventures. The rest of the master poem takes place on Odysseus' home isle of Ithaca. What is most puzzling is that when Odysseus finally does arrive, he is asleep and unconscious. When he awakes, he does not recognize where he is. Home is strange. His beloved Ithaca is disguised. As he struggles to regain home, he appears as a stranger in his own land, in the guise of a ragged old beggar man. When asked, "Who are you? Where do you come from?" he lies, deceives, and confabulates. One would expect a majestic, returning hero to reveal himself in homecoming glory, but Odysseus does not. Even after he does reveal himself to his son, nurse, swineherd, and wife in turn, he almost cruelly hides his identity from his pining, elderly father, Laertes. Why does Odysseus come home deliberately disguising himself as a stranger?

The reason given within the *Odyssey* for Odysseus' deception is self-protection. Greedy suitors have invaded Odysseus' house and plan to force his wife to marry one of them. They are actively conspiring to kill his son, Telemachos, the one male threat to their plot. If Laertes' son was discovered, undisguised, those recklessly greedy young men might well murder him. This is reason he gives his son, nurse, and swineherd, but we know that Odysseus is an ever-crafty, unreliable, super-trickster. In Homer, Odysseus is described as, *polytropos,* a man of many plans and deceits—cunning, resourceful, resilient, never at a loss. For a *polytropos,* can one ever take his reason at face value? Are there not deeper reasons that connect homecoming with disguise?

Surprisingly, many traditions link disguise and homecoming. In the Indian epic, the *Mahabharata,* the five Pandava brothers must spend an entire year in disguise before they are allowed to return home. In the Bible, the stories of Abraham, Isaac, Jacob, Joseph, Judah, and Tamar, as well as David, all involve the theme of disguise, trickery, and exile/homecoming. Superman is a modern superhero whose life story is also based on the double identity as Superman and Clark Kent. It is played out against the impossibility of homecoming since Superman's native world was destroyed. At the last moment, his father rocketed him to safety. Significantly, the one thing that endangers Superman's magical powers and life force is kryptonite, the remnant of his annihilated homeland. For exiles who have remade themselves into a powerful new assimilated identity, any contact with the lost home can be undermining, even deadly. These Indian, Biblical, Greek, and superhero stories suggest there does exist an archetypal pattern involving danger, disguise, and homecoming.

The *Odyssey* is the sequel to the *Iliad* where Odysseus first appears. The *Iliad* is the seemingly endless, epic struggle between the Trojans and the Greeks. As an epic, the *Iliad* is based on the values of the first half of life, what Homer called *kleos*, lasting fame and heroic glory. For warriors, glory matters most. Within that world of *kleos*, there is no possibility of a real homecoming. The end of one war is only the prelude to the next, as Odysseus himself describes in one of his false cover stories. Perhaps that is why the *Iliad* ends with the struggle for Troy unresolved, reflecting the emotional reality of the warrior's masculine identity that is never resolved. A young masculine hero needs to prove and re-prove that he is a "real man" over and over. The *Iliad's* ending may be understood as a subtle, moral critique of the hero myth. Heroic values take one away from home, but they cannot bring one back. It is impossible to come home solely through the masculine values of bravery, strength, and courage. Ironically, only in the *Odyssey*, does one learn that it is not courage or *kleos* that brings victory to the Greeks, but Odysseus' cunning.

Although the epic is named for Odysseus, he does not make his actual debut until the fifth book of the *Odyssey*. His fame, however, goes before him. Helen, (whose beauty triggered the Trojan War) makes the most successful (and improbable) homecoming. When Odysseus' son comes looking for word of his father, she slips her husband and Odysseus' son, Telemachus, an ancient, tranquilizing wine, drugged with an herb that banishes all care and sorrow. She then tells of how she met Odysseus inside the walls of Troy, covered with wounds and bruises and dressed in rags, but he was really a spy in disguise. (Ironically, this disguise is very similar to how Odysseus will arrive at Ithaca.) Only Helen recognized him. But Odysseus was too cunning for her. He forced her to swear a solemn oath not to betray him till he had returned safely to his own camp. Helen washed, anointed and gave him new clothes, fore-shadowing the process of renewal of his persona in his subsequent homecoming.

Helen's husband, Menelaus, then tells the story of how Odysseus invented an enormous hollow horse large enough to conceal a Greek fighting force that was brought to the gates of Troy as a "gift from the gods." The Trojans, uncertain whether the horse is Greek or Divine sent Helen to examine the horse. Helen, a sophisticated tricksteress in her own right, devises a test based on a fighting man's yearning for wife and home. She walks round the wooden structure and imitates the voice of the wives of each Greek hiding inside. As each armed man is about to respond to Helen's impersonation, Odysseus clamps shut their mouth and saves them all from premature exposure. Odysseus' role is to suppress those nostalgic feelings that if expressed at the wrong time, can be fatal for the warrior.

The Jungian perspective on Odysseus usually sees him as an irrepressible trickster-warrior who must encounter the feminine.[15] Without the help of his lover-goddesses, first Calypso and then Circe, Odysseus would never come home but die the death of a lonely refugee. The first glimpse the epic gives of Odysseus on the isle of the goddess Calypso, with whom he has lived for seven years, stridently sets the theme. He is sitting on the seashore weeping, suffering severe nostalgia. Nostalgia, "a painful yearning for home," is a condition first used to describe Swiss exiles who suffered torment because they were far from their mountain homeland. A yearning for home, we now know, is a pan-human condition. Homesickness reflects person's longing for a certain existential space that bears the imprint of home. The Chinese poet Li Po gives exquisite expression to this longing. His poem begins:

Before my bed there is bright moonlight
So that it seems like frost on the ground:

Then concludes:

> Lifting my head I watch the bright moon,
> Lowering my head I dream that I'm home.[16]

The phrase "I dream that I am home" touches the soul of anyone on the road, whether traveler, migrant, exile, or refugee. We are always dreaming of home (even sometimes when we are at home).

Home is not only a physical location but also cluster of feelings associated with a specific place. These feelings may include a *participation mystique* attachment to nature, soil, childhood, customs, community, a way of thinking, dress, food, and so on. Wittgenstein might argue that it is difficult to say clearly what home is exactly, yet one can point to it. Home resembles the "home base" in a children's game, a place of absolute safety, where no harm can touch us. It is like "home plate" in baseball, the place where we start from and where we seek to go: our origin and our destination, from our first home in mother's womb to the last home on Mother Earth. A haiku by that famous Japanese wanderer, Basho, expresses the bonding between origin and homecoming. The haiku begins:

> Coming home at last
> At the end of the year

Then concludes:

I wept to find
My old umbilical cord.[17]

At his Tower in Bollingen, Jung felt "in midst of my true life, I am most deeply myself."[18] Home provides a natural container for the Self. When I am feeling most grounded, most centered, most understood, most at peace, most "at home," there is home. The German language has an especially rich vocabulary concerning relationship to home: *heimat,* means home or homeland but really much more; *heimatliebe,* love for home; *heimattreue,* being true to home/homeland; *heimatgefühl,* feeling of attachment to home; and *heimatort,* place where ancestors became citizen. The Chinese ideogram for home is said to represent a roof over a pig, since nothing is at home as a pig in its sty. We are most ourselves when we are most at home.

Archetypal experience of home includes the security, protection, nest warmth, and the food base of the mother, as well as the boundaried, division of inner and outer, belonging to the father. This tension between these masculine and feminine aspects of home is well expressed in a poem by Robert Frost.[19] A farmer's wife tells her husband that a wayward hired hand has come home to die. The farmer responds, "It all depends on what you mean by home." He continues with what is one of Frost's most famous lines:

> Home is the place where, when you have
> to go there,
> They have to take you in.

The farmer's view epitomizes a masculine view of home as a necessary, ultimate refuge. It is the home of last resort, where duty and logos reign. His wife, speaking in the feminine voice, counters that home is "Something you somehow haven't to deserve." Home is one's emotional birthright, the realm of unconditionally accepting *eros*. As the seat of the Self, home is therefore strongly protecting and accepting, requiring and nurturing, strong walls around the warmth of the hearth. It is intensely masculine and profoundly feminine. For home, or indeed a therapeutic space, to work, all these opposites need to be held together well.

The dilemma arises when we leave home. How do we hold on to "home" when we leave it? We carry within us an internal "home image" which links and roots us in home while we are away. Some cultures use a special ceremony to permanently (through ritual) root a person in their home soil. The Betsimisaraka are a people who live in the rainforest of the east coast of Madagascar.[20] After birth, the placental expulsion, or afterbirth, is buried immediately adjacent to their very simple hut (made entirely from the "Traveler's Plant"):

one side for girls, the other for boys. The placenta, which had served as the baby's first home is buried into the earth, the domain of the powerful ancestors. It provides an existential grounding for the person's soul. The Betsimisaraka claim that not to bury the afterbirth risks madness, a condition they conceptualize as ungrounded homelessness. These Malagasy people believe that to forget or be detached from the homeland is a kind of madness. Yet, it is just such an anti-nostalgic "homenesia" or amnesia for home, that threatens Odysseus and his men again and again during their circuitous voyage. The men who eat of the lotus are like drug addicts who forget where they are going and where they have come from and become rooted in the homelessness of the present. The madness of home-forgetting recurs repeatedly in the Odyssey. When Circe's magic turns men into pigs, Odysseus forgets his destination for a full year, and again for even longer, when seduced by the charming Calypso. These stories of seduction reveal the ever-present danger concerning homecoming, namely, that settling into a cozy existence, one forgets there is a home to come home to.

Once a homecomer does return, he faces a double anxiety.[21] He yearns to return to the exact home he had left behind, crystallized in an idealized image of home. Yet, inevitably, he will find that home has changed. How the homecomer copes with those home changes will largely determine the success of the fundamental project of returning home. In the background, there is a silent terror that the home he knew is gone: distorted, betrayed, or even lost forever. No wonder the process of homecoming can be so long and complicated, as it was for Odysseus.

One such well-known complication is reverse culture shock. Most people expect to feel culture shock when they travel to strange locations, but few expect to feel strange when they return home, as Odysseus does. It is doubly disorienting because the unexpected sense of strangeness is embedded in an expectation of familiarity. I expect to feel at home, but I do not. The difficulty of reverse culture shock in the process of homecoming is poignantly illustrated in the tragic story of Honi, a Talmudic Rip van Winkle.[22] The story begins that one day, Honi saw a man planting a carob tree:
"How many years does it take for this tree to bear fruit?" he asked the man.
"Seventy years."
"Do you think you will live seventy more years?"
The man replied, "I found a world containing carob trees, and just as my ancestors planted those trees for me, so too will I plant them for my descendants."
Honi sat down and drowsiness overcame him and he fell asleep. Some rocks rose to cover him, and he became hidden from sight.
He slept for seventy years, and when he woke up, he saw what looked to be the same man picking fruit from the carob tree he had planted.

Honi asked him, "Are you the man who planted this tree?"

"No, I am his grandson."

Honi said, "I must have slept for seventy years."

He went to his home village and asked, "Is the son of Honi still alive?"

He was told him, "His son is no longer alive, but his grandson is."

He said to them, "I am Honi."

They didn't believe him.

He left and went to the house of study (*beit hamidrash*) where he heard a rabbi speaking about his wisdom and teachings.

Honi said to them, "I am Honi."

They did not believe him and did not treat him with the honor and respect due him.

Honi became anguished. He prayed for death and died. The editor adds: Hence the saying, "Either friendship or death." Honi was not able to fight his way past these strangers who had taken over his home. Left on the outside, looking in, his life lost its meaning. From this perspective, one can understand Odysseus' determination to fight his way home.

Claire Cooper Marcus who wrote an imaginative and insightful book, *House as a Mirror of Self: Exploring the Deeper Meaning of Home*, tells how she came to write the book. Her sudden divorce left her feeling a "profound degree of insecurity, pain, grief, and anger, all rolled into one," which profoundly changed her experience of her own home. She became terrified that someone would break in and kill her and her children. She had to symbolically fight her way through it and retake home. Once she had succeeded, home again became a place that "can protect, heal, and restore us, express who we are now, and over time, help us to become who we are meant to be."[23]

It is important to recall why Odysseus' return sea voyage took so long. Odysseus and his crew arrived at the island of the one-eyed Cyclops, where one of these giants devoured six of Odysseus' men. To save himself and the rest of his men, Odysseus tricked the man-eating monster into drinking sufficient wine until he was dead drunk, rather like Laius or Lot. With great passion, Odysseus drove a fire-hardened stake deep into the giant's eye, blinding him. There is a comic element. Odysseus had introduced himself as "No one," so when the blinded giant awoke, he cried out, "No one has blinded me." Brutality and burlesque. Once Odysseus escaped, he revealed his true name to the Cyclops in a misguided bravado of *kleos*. For this hubris, Odysseus paid dearly. The blinded Cyclops prayed to his father, Poseidon, Lord of the Waters to avenge the wound, so that Odysseus would never return home, or if he did, it would be without any ship or any crew companions. For the entire homeward journey, Odysseus had to sail and struggle against this curse. From a symbolic perspective, Odysseus' act can be seen as a sin against consciousness (symbolized by the eye), and in violation of the collective unconscious (symbolized by the sea). It is Odysseus' own lack of consciousness, which repeatedly prevents him from returning to Ithaca. When almost in sight of home, he falls asleep, allowing his greedy men to open the bag of winds and send their ship into swift reverse. At two other times, a similar sleepy unconsciousness allowed his men to violate the sacred order by pillaging, or by eating the sacred cattle of the Sun. Odysseus' men act like an autonomous, impulsive complex, unconstrained by ego awareness. Only after his last total shipwreck, where he has washed up alone and told his story, does he fall into a different and deepening sleep.

There are other, shadow homecomings that haunt Odysseus. The most horrific is Agamemnon's. Agamemnon, the commander-in-chief of the victorious Greeks, returns, only to be murdered by his wife and her lover. Instead of a place of primal safety, home for Agamemnon is the most dangerous place on earth. His wife is waiting for him, not with an embrace, but a dagger. How does Odysseus know that his Penelope is not waiting to do the same?

The reader knows that Penelope is the embodiment of a faithful wife, weaving by day and unweaving by night to keep her marriage safe. But Penelope herself has a dilemma. Penelope's conflict with the suitors (and herself) is whether she is an *aguna*. An *aguna*, in Jewish tradition, is a woman whose husband has disappeared without firm evidence that he is definitely dead, and literally means "a woman chained to her marriage." She is forbidden to divorce, mourn, or remarry. The *aguna* is, therefore, someone in marital limbo. Civil law allows one to eventually declare a missing spouse legally "dead" and free an *aguna*. Such an option does not exist in Jewish religious law.

Penelope is an *aguna*; Odysseus is an MIA, missing-in-action. MIA families also live in agonizing limbo of perennial anxiety of homecoming. Will he come home, or not? Will I never know his fate? To mourn the missing father/spouse/brother/son is to betray him and hope; not to mourn is to live a life on permanent hold, to be a symbolic, if not a literal, *aguna*. Those who never come home represent a serious, collective danger. These unincorporated dead become hungry, wandering, restless ghosts, who pose a symbolic danger to the social order. Their unresolved fates, like those of Odysseus' shipmates, represent a chaotic destructive force from the collective unconscious. They pursue the memories of the living, demanding recognition, demanding their share, and if forgotten, seeking revenge. The Betsimisaraka, mentioned above, understand this dilemma well. They carve a simple wooden sculpture in the shape of a "standing man" for those whose bodies are never found. These statues stand for the bones of the deceased and provide their spirit a place to reside where they may be nurtured and contacted by the living. In this context, one can understand the importance of the Tomb of the Unknown Soldier. These massive constructions serve as repositories not only for the bones of "soldiers known only to God" but also for their wandering souls. These Tombs gives them a space to which they may come home and so let themselves, and us, rest in peace.

When Odysseus reveals his husband-identity to his wife, Penelope, one would expect Penelope to rush over to welcome her long-absent husband. She does not. Instead, she is frozen, numb, silent, sitting opposite him, unmoving. The scene depicts what I call the Martin Guerre dilemma, based on an extraordinary case of disguise in 16th century France and made into the celebrated movie, *The Return of Martin Guerre*.[24] A man, calling himself Martin Guerre returns from the wars and is accepted by Martin Guerre's wife. They even have two children together. Ultimately, doubts appear about his identity and the man is charged with fraud as an imposter. His trial continues, until, at the very last minute, the real Martin Guerre dramatically appears, exposing the counterfeit husband. One of the poignant questions is at what point did Martin Guerre's wife know that the imposter was a fraud, especially since the imposter was a more sensitive and loving husband than her original husband, who was more than a bit of a brute. The film, subtly, replays Penelope's dilemma: How can a wife know if the man who returns from the wars in those filthy rags is really her lost love, or a sophisticated fraudster? The Martin Guerre dilemma is not limited to romantic reconciliations. It may apply to any situation whenever recognition is at risk.

After this first meeting, Odysseus avoids his wife. Instead, he plans new deceptions in order to gain time before the inevitable, revenge attack by the relatives of the massacred suitors. Odysseus, bathed, oiled, and dressed, as he had with Helen, now reemerges in his restored persona, "looking more like a god than a man." He confronts his wife again. Still she does not respond. Odysseus calls her an unfeeling woman, with a heart of steel. In frustration, he asks his old nurse to prepare a bed for him to sleep alone. His request gives Penelope her chance to resolve the Martin Guerre paradox.

Penelope, trickster in her own right, needs to discover if this man knows secrets known only to her husband. Penelope, casually, asks the old nurse to make up their marriage bed for Odysseus outside the bedchamber. The bed, handcrafted by Odysseus out of a living olive tree, cannot be moved. Only Odysseus knows this unmovable secret. How does he respond? Odysseus, for the first and only time in the entire epic, loses his cool. He becomes angry, claiming no living man can move such a bed. Why did Odysseus, normally so restrained, become enraged? The living marriage bed was a crucial part of Odysseus' home image, which sustained him during those years of wandering homelessness. To lose the bed is to lose the sacred center of their home: to have no wife and home to return to. Odysseus, knowing the bed secret, regains his wife, his home and his identity. Penelope melts. She rushes to her husband and confesses she feared he was an imposter. Odysseus, the great trickster, is tricked by his own trickster wife, into revealing who he really is.

One might think that this moment of unmasking brings the Odyssey to its natural endings. But there is one more, exquisitely painful episode of homecoming anxiety. Odysseus visits his aged father and finds him pruning trees in the country. He wonders if his father will know him when he sees him. When he spies his father, Odysseus, with tears in his eyes, wonders what should he do? Should he throw his arms around him, kiss and tell him the whole story of his homecoming or not? Odysseus, too, is in the Martin Guerre dilemma. He decides to pretend to be someone else. This episode has puzzled readers and scholars alike who have difficulty understanding Odysseus' seemingly cruel deception. Yet it makes sense within the logic of disguise as a pathway to homecoming. Only if Odysseus is masked, can he be unmasked. Consider the shadow scenario. Odysseus rushes up to the father, who refuses to believe the embracing one is his returning son. Eventually, he does say to his father, "I am the man you are looking for." He reveals the thigh wound, the names of the trees promised to him in childhood as the indisputable signs of his true identity.

After he has come home, reunited with son, wife, and father, Odysseus must perform one final act of penance to reconcile with angry Poseidon. On his voyage to the Underworld, the prophet Tiresias commanded him to take an oar on his shoulder from his ship and to walk inland until a person will ask, "Why are you carrying a winnowing paddle?" At that exact spot in a land that knows nothing of the sea, or sea salt, Odysseus must build a Temple to the Lord of the Waters and offer him sacrifices. Then his trials will be over and he can come home to a comfortable old age and an easy death.

How can one understand this strange penance? Odysseus' deliberately blinding the Sea God's son in symbolic terms can be seen as destructive act toward consciousness. His actions with the oar can be therefore understood as representing an expansion of consciousness. He brings Poseidon-like energy into a new territory of the psyche. Odysseus' last odyssey brings together not only land and sea but also surface and depth, knowing and unknowing, and even sin and forgiveness. Having gone so far into unknown territory, he can finally come home.

Why Socrates Remembered

Socrates' final day is the most famous deathbed scene in Western civilization.[25] It remains the archetypal account of how a true philosopher can face death, even such an unjust, judicial murder, with inner calm. It was, and is, the very paradigm of a good death. Socrates faces his execution with the clear belief that he is going to a better, more ideal, existence. He maintains his dignity throughout and disapproves of any showy emotion. Socrates deliberately sends away his wife and children when they become too emotional and he chastises his disciples when they, too, weep. Plato himself cannot even bear to attend.

Socrates drinks the hemlock poison, and starts feeling the effects of the poison. His feet, legs, and then his groin, go numb and cold, in turn. Just then, Socrates suddenly remembers. He uncovers his face and says, "Crito, I owe a cock to Asclepius; will you remember to pay the debt?" These are Socrates' last words. Many attempts have been made to try to understand the significance of these unexpected last words. One scholar lists twenty-one distinct interpretations.[26] Clearly, there is no consensus on the meaning of the enigmatic request. Some see Socrates as the most responsible of men, careful to pay all his literal and symbolic debts to Asclepius, the god of healing. Others see his words as having profound metaphorical or philosophic significance. This is Nietzsche's view, when he has Socrates say, "Oh Crito, Life is a disease."[27] Therefore, death is the cure for the disease called of life.

Most explanations, however, fail to appreciate how puzzling Socrates' statement really is. In the hours just prior to the deathbed scene, Socrates takes a bath to spare the need of the women to wash his corpse. At that time, Crito asked his beloved teacher, "And have you any commands for us, Socrates—anything to say about your children, or any other matter in which we can serve you?" Socrates replies that he has nothing particular in mind, only to take care of yourselves.[28] After Socrates has swallowed the hemlock, Crito told Socrates that the executioner has requested that he speak as little as possible, since speech may interfere with the action of the poison. How is it that only a short while later at the last moment of consciousness, Socrates suddenly remembers his sacred obligation? Crito agrees to give the rooster to Asclepius and then asks, "Is there anything else?" But Socrates can no longer speak. A moment later, he is dead. If Socrates so desired to live his life correctly, why did he wait so long to ask that this outstanding debt be paid? The question must therefore be asked: Why did

Socrates not mention the debt to Asclepius when Crito asked the first time just before the bath? And what caused Socrates to suddenly remember?

To answer these questions, first we need to examine Socrates' view of the body. Socrates, as is well known, had a stridently negative attitude toward the body. Earlier in his Phaedo dialogue, he makes his position crystal clear:

> The philosopher desires death...
> What is the nature of that death which he desires?

He continues:

> Death is the separation of soul and body—and the philosopher desires such a separation. He would like to be freed from the dominion of bodily pleasures and of the senses, which are always perturbing his mental vision.

And concludes:

> He wants to get rid of eyes and ears, and with the light of the mind only to behold the light of truth. All the evils and impurities and necessities of men come from the body...

For the philosopher, the soul is compared to a helpless prisoner chained hand and foot to the body. A philosopher will be only happy to be free of it. The transition to death to eternal forms should be joyous.

The context in which his last words were spoken is while the poison had begun to take effect. Here is the full text of Socrates' dying:

> He was beginning to grow cold about the groin, when he uncovered his face, for he had covered himself up, and said—they were his last words—he said: Crito, I owe a cock to Asclepius; will you remember to pay the debt?

> Crito responds:

> The debt shall be paid... is there anything else? There was no answer to this question; but in a minute or two a movement was heard, and the attendants uncovered him; his eyes were set, and Crito closed his eyes and mouth.

The key to Socrates' remembering seems to be in its timing. The poison renders Socrates insensitive and cold, first in his feet, then along his legs and finally within his groin; it is at this point that he dramatically uncovers his face and speaks. Something in his bodily experience of the effects of the poison led him to remember the debt he owed. When a physical sensation brings something long forgotten to mind, it is called a "somatic memory."

Somatic memories typically result from traumatic experiences that overload our mental capacities to contain them. When the emotional pain is so intense, the mind cannot absorb it and it blows the mental circuit breaker so that the memories are stored, not in the mind, but in the body. The traumatic memory overflows from the mind into the body, leaving a memory blackout. There is no conscious recall of the trauma, yet the body remembers. Sometimes, some specific sensation will retrigger the lost memory. For example, a woman is sexually abused as a child, but has no memory of the incident. Years later, during sexual intercourse, her hand is accidentally pinned down behind the pillow just as it was during the initial abuse. The experience triggers strange and disturbing intrusive experiences such as flashbacks, dissociations or out of body experiences, indicative of the memory of the sexual trauma breaking through into consciousness. Later, she has disturbing dreams. Gradually, the evil deed returns from the body back into the mind.

Phantom limb is another kind of body memory that does not let go. A limb has been amputated and is no longer part of the body. But amputees very often experience pain in the leg or arm they no longer have. Somatic memories are most closely associated with trauma and may occur in serious illness experience, as well. For Socrates, I believe, the poison triggered a body memory of a physically and emotionally difficult disease connected to the groin area. It is a cliché that doctors make the worst patients but I suspect that philosophers like Socrates, with their over-emphasis on rationality and logos, may be even worse. Socrates' overvaluing the soul and undervaluing the body comes at a price. Every illness forces us to inhabit our body intensely. It is hard to dwell on the ideal when you are devoured by itch, nausea, or mind-bending pain. Illness is the body's revenge of the body on philosophers and idealists. That revenge may well have come to Socrates when the body in compensation demanded its share. In my reconstruction, I believe Socrates, once in his life, while suffering severe physical pain and dis-ease, impulsively promised to offer a rooster to the god of healing, if only that he should escape from the body's clutching vise. The intensity of the illness experience overflowed from his exquisite mind directly into a somatic experience. When Socrates recovered, he regained his philosophical poise. He once again idealized the spirit and devalued the body. He forgot the agonies of his own disease experience and did what he would never justify: he broke his promise.

Talmud says that a dream uninterpreted is like a letter unopened.[29] Jung believed that repeating dreams signal that the letter has not been opened. Socrates himself had such a repeating dream:

In the course of my life I have often had intimations in dreams 'that I should compose music.' The same dream came to me sometimes in one form, and sometimes in another, but always saying the same or nearly the same words: 'Cultivate and make music,' said the dream.

Reflecting on the dream, Socrates saw the dream as encouragement of his way of life:

And hitherto I had imagined that this was only intended to exhort and encourage me in the study of philosophy, which has been the pursuit of my life, and is the noblest and best of music. The dream was bidding me do what I was already doing, in the same way that the competitor in a race is bidden by the spectators to run when he is already running.

Jung taught that dreams must be telling us something new and now Socrates had doubts:

But I was not certain of this, for the dream might have meant music in the popular sense of the word, and being

under sentence of death, and the festival
giving me a respite, I thought that it
would be safer for me to satisfy the
scruple, and, in obedience to the dream,
to compose a few verses before I
departed. And first I made a hymn in
honour of the god of the festival, and then
considering that a poet, if he is really to
be a poet, should not only put together
words, but should invent stories, and that
I have no invention, I took some fables of
Aesop, which I had ready at hand and
which I knew—they were the first I came
upon—and turned them into verse.

Jung taught that a repeating dream is an urgent
communication to the conscious mind from the
unconscious. The dream recurs precisely because it has
not been understood or integrated. It was a type of dream
that Jung understood. Individuals with post-traumatic
stress disorder—PTSD—often have such nightly,
repetitive nightmares. The psyche relentlessly takes the
dreamer back to where the healing must begin. It is
rather like parent needing to cleanse a wound of a child
who screams "No! No!" But returning to the wound is
the only way to allow the natural process of healing to
begin.

Socrates in prison, on death row, realizes that he has misunderstood the dream. He thought it was encouraging him to pursue philosophy, which he understood as divine music. The Jungian approach is that a dream must always tell you something new, something you do not know, or do not know well enough. Socrates now understands the dream is not symbolic, but quite literal and "objective." He decided to begin composing verse and developing the neglected, inferior yet creative side of his personality. The Greek god of music and poetry was Apollo, the father of Asclepius, the god of healing. Music is an art form that must be experienced via the senses. Music may be divine, but it needs to be heard through the body to be appreciated. Socrates' philosophy is an introverted thinking style which seeks to escape the world, while music stimulates inner and outer at the same time. Each one of us must come to terms with the discontinuity between matter and spirit; between flesh and soul. When I shut my eyes alone in a quieted room, I can easily imagine myself without a body in Socratic realm of pure thought. One can listen to music and do philosophy with one's eyes closed. Any decisive pain, however, will rapidly bring a person back down into their body. True, meditation, yoga, stoical attitude, and other techniques may restore an inner sense of serenity. But the pain sensation as part of the body baggage does not disappear, only the evaluation of it: "I am in excruciating agony. How interesting!"

Socrates' request raises another concern deeply neglected by contemporary medicine, and that is the issue of an "end of the illness" ritual. Medical sociology has much to say how people enter the sick role, especially when they do it too early (cybersomatics), or too late (anorexics, alcoholics), or settle in too comfortably into their secondary gain. There is much investigation of how illness begins, but very little on how it ends. Modern medical life lacks those re-integrating ceremonies, so common in traditional societies that ritually welcome the sick back into the community and into health. Socrates, in his many dialogues, does speak positively of physicians. According to the Xenophon,[30] for example, Socrates urged his companions to take care of their health, to learn as much as they can from "those who know" and what sorts of meat, drink, and exercise are best for their constitutions. Socrates, in this advice, sounds like the "good patient" who recognizes the authority of the physician over the body. He understood the importance of being an active participant in the "primary prevention" of disease through living a healthy lifestyle.

Benjamin Franklin said, "God cures and the physician collects the fee." In ancient Greece, the gods always collected their fee. The fee was collected via a formal offering of thanksgiving to the god of healing. These offerings served as an "end of illness" ritual that marked a formal return to a life of health and wholeness. Judaism in its current form lacks animal sacrifice, but it has a ritual that marks the end of illness. The ritual, called

Birkat HaGomel, is a Blessing of Deliverance, recited publicly in a synagogue.[31] It is said by anyone, following a subjective experience of being "saved" from danger, including a serious illness.[32] It is a public declaration that the danger is over. *HaGomel* is what that great student of rites of passage, Arnold van Gennep, called a ritual of reincorporation. The sick are segregated from society in special places, such as the hospital or the sanitarium. Patients are forced to give up everyday dress, and wear demeaning hospital gowns that reveal their dependent, diminished status. As patients lie between recovery and death, they undergo diverse restrictions: they are required either to eat special foods, or not to eat at all; they are forced to move, or are not allowed to do so. Such extremes are characteristic of the liminal phase of rites of passage in which one is between old and new status, neither here nor there. When an observant Jewish patient recovers, and gives the prayer of *HaGomel,* the congregation affirms the blessing but also recognizes the individual's reincorporation as a full member of the community of the healthy.

Contemporary medicine offers no such rite of passage on leaving the hospital. After an operation or heart attack, a patient's departure is distressingly banal and bureaucratic. There is no formal watershed to draw the existential line between the illness that was, and the new unfolding recovery that will be. There is no community ritual celebrating the end of danger. Without such a ritual of thanksgiving, the modern patient does not make the true transition to be reborn in health. Instead, one is symbolically trapped in that liminal space between ease and dis-ease.

Socrates clearly understood that the transition from illness to health must be marked and accounted for. In Greek culture, the way one showed gratitude was the killing of a defenseless animal. How can such an act of deliberate cruelty serve as a ritual marker? Precisely because a holy act of slaughter marked the boundary between life and death. One moment the animal was alive and the next moment, it was dead. The rooster would have crossed over, had the debt been paid before; Socrates had stayed behind. Now it was Socrates' time to cross over. Death is the time when we have to pay up our debts. For Socrates, death was not the dying of the light, but a rite of passage into "a better place." He would have agreed with the John Donne: *One short sleep past, we wake eternally.*[33] Rites of passage, as we have seen, draw a line between who we were and who we will become. Socrates was no longer who he had been, but was not yet who he hoped he would be. The danger is that one will not make the transition but be locked, like a wandering ghost in that liminal space. Just as he had not truly passed from sickness to health, so too, he might not pass from death to Eternal Life. At that last moment of his life, Socrates had to give the body its due.

WHY DO MEN WEAR TIES?

The next time you see someone dressed in a business suit, ask yourself, "Why **do** men wear ties?" Ties are enormously familiar and yet in another sense, they are strangely exotic and bizarre. Neckties are the required part of the code of dress for everyone sporting a white collar. How odd to have this decorated piece of cloth dangling in front, pointing directly down toward the genitals. Clothes are an important and dynamic form of nonverbal communication. What is the significance of this "useless bit of coloured cloth tied in a complicated way, and which makes it harder to get air into your lungs and difficult to turn your neck"[34]? Men in tribal societies often wear elaborate and dramatically eye-catching costumes. New Guinea Highlanders or Wodaabe people of the Sahara are world leaders in the flashy male look. But each element in their appearance is highly semiotic, drenched with significance. Hundreds of million men put on ties every day. Do they ask themselves: why am I wearing a tie? What does it say about being a man? What is the meaning of neckties?

Given the zeitgeist of transparency, I want to first to disclose my own relation to neckties. Throughout high school, it was compulsory to wear a white shirt and tie (no jacket). I still have vivid memories of a circular rotating tie holder which hung in my closet, from which I would select the day's tie—a knitted dark blue one stands out in my memory, as I finger its ruffled, three-dimensional texture, to decide whether today is its day.

When I was accepted to Yale College, I was informed that neckties, although not required for classes, were obligatory to enter the dining room of our colleges. It was the sixties. Rebels quickly undermined the "tie rule" by appearing in tee shirts and ties, until the rule was quietly dropped the following year. The irony was that the rule had only been introduced about ten years previously. Prior to that time, there was no need for the "tie rule," since Yalies automatically put on ties as regularly as their investment banker fathers had.

Since then, neckties and I have parted ways. One thing I enjoy about living in Israel is that few people wear ties, even at weddings or other formal occasions. In contrast, in Croatia, ties are **only** likely to be worn at life cycle rites of passage: christenings, weddings, and funerals.[35] I do remember the last time I wore a tie. It was in Zurich at the Congress of my professional organization, International Association of Analytical Psychology. A dear friend had bought me a lavish, silky broad-faced tie in honor of our friendship. I thought here I would wear it in his honor at the Closing Banquet. I had arranged to go with analyst friend from San Francisco. When I started to tie the knot, I realized I had forgotten that specific motor skill, despite Oscar Wilde's remark that a well-tied tie is the first serious step in life. My analyst friend stood over me from behind and adeptly tied me up saying it reminded him of days long past, initiating his sons into the rite of tying. Later, when I got back to the hotel, I was so happy to take it off, and it has stayed off. I find tie-wearing fascinating, but I hope I never have to wear one again.

Neckties have a long and distinguished military history. The "terracotta" soldiers in the army of China's first emperor, uncovered in Xi'an, have neckties. Roman orators used neckerchiefs to keep their vocal chords warm. Most historians trace the origin of the modern necktie to an elite Croatian army unit presented to Louis XIV's France in 1650. Their distinctive uniform included a Croatian scarf, derived from the word for "Croat," the French called "la cravate." Later, another French military unit fighting at the Battle of Steinkirke did not have time to get dressed properly in the rush to battle and tucked their scarves into their buttonholes. The "steinkirke," a neck cloth with long laces, became popular. In 1880, Oxford University rowers from Exeter College undid their hatbands and tied them 'round their necks. The first school tie was created. Elite military units, social clubs, colleges, and branches of law enforcement still have their own distinctive ties.

The military origins of neckties suggest that they are first and foremost part of a uniform. It shows that tie-wearers have accepted the key ground rules for what is acceptable in white collar, masculine behavior. They display values of conformity, identity, and belonging. If one sees someone wearing a tie, their social status is apparent. Men who wear ties do not work with their hands. They rarely work outdoors like a lineman, miner, or cowboy does. Tie-wearers are "reliable." Their god is Apollo and they will never do something Dionysian, at least not with their ties on. The tie displays that the wearer is tied, tied to the social role of being a male executive/diplomat/professional, bound to the role he is playing. Ties are all about power. People with ties tell people without ties what to do.

Visually, the tie with its bulging knot serves to exaggerate the Adam's apple. The Adam's apple is a laryngeal prominence made of cartilage that surrounds the larynx. It is stimulated by hormones during adolescence and is a significant secondary sexual characteristic in males, associated with the deepening of the voice. It is misnamed for the apple Adam is alleged to have swallowed in the Garden of Eden, which stuck in his throat. Despite the popular notion that the apple was the fruit of the tree of the knowledge of good and evil, the identification is undoubtedly mistaken. Apples are not native to the Middle East. By internal evidence and according to ancient Hebrew traditions, figs are a much more likely candidate. Perhaps one ought to say, "Adam's fig." In any case, despite the name, the symbolism of Adam's apple is not elaborated.

The knot that highlights the Adam's apple serves to exaggerate the masculinity of the wearer, just as shoulder pads do for American footballers. At the same time, it is a masculinity that is constricted and constrained, one that is tied up. This dilemma of needing to be hyper-masculine, and yet tied up within a hierarchy that demands conformity and submission, is one experienced by every corporate manager and bureaucrat.

Ties also divide the body into two: above the tie and below the tie. Freud claimed that ties in dreams are symbols of the penis. I believe that ties point more upward than downward, to emphasize the head at the expense of the body. Ties are worn by those who work with their heads. The tight neck division between head and body can have its cost. A tight tie can cause the internal pressure of the eye to rise, leading to glaucoma, a leading cause of blindness. Glaucoma is a serious medical condition, but it also seems like a metaphor for what can happen when the necktie is symbolically too tight, namely, a loss of vision and an absence of insight.

At many international gatherings, whether political or commercial, men tend to look very similar. Each wears a suit and a tie. There are two places, however, where neckties are not welcome. One is the Islamic Republic of Iran and the other is in British hospitals. Iranian Islamic leadership forbade neckties as an evil import from the imperialist West. The former president of Iran's trademark was a jacket with an open collar. Tielessness was a symbol of being free and untied to the West with its un-Islamic values. If the Iranian ban on ties is symbolic politics, then the hospital ban is entirely practical. Numerous studies have shown that ties are germ-laden. One study showed that at least half of the physicians' ties contained disease-causing microorganisms, including potentially deadly

Staphylococcus aureus or *Aspergillus*. Five to ten percent of all hospital patients acquire infections while in the hospital, which leads to 90,000 deaths and 4.5 billion dollars in costs. Doctors are much less likely to dry clean a tie than their white shirt. As one physician put it, "You come home and throw the tie on the tie rack and a week later you wear it again. It's rarely clean." Although no specific death has been linked to a tie, the British Medical Association banned ties and the AMA is considering doing the same. Some physicians and patients are not happy with the ban on ties as it challenges the image of the authority of a physician.

Recently, Richard Branson allowed the newest group of Virgin employees to dispose of ties, saying that he had always hated ties since they were uncomfortable and serve no useful purpose. Given the absurdity of neckties, one wonders why a masculine world that prides itself on rationality and logos, insists on something so lacking any clear function. But perhaps, that is the actual, secret meaning of ties. They are the crucial symbol that, even in a world of conformity, suppression of individuality, and profit and loss, there must be a place for the irrational. Women's dresses have an enormous range of display possibilities. A dress can be almost any color or length, or degree of decoration and texture. This fascinating array of fashion possibility is often accompanied by an unfair amount of persona anxiety. Women ask themselves and others: "How do I look?" Male work attire, in contrast, is highly standardized. The striking absence of variation or adornment makes modern men so very different from their male counterparts in the rest of the animal kingdom, who are given to proclaim: "Hey, look at me!" Given the limited repertoire of the formal dress code, neckties can be seen to take on an enormous, expressive importance. Ties offer the male a unique focus for personal expression.

Neckties, like dresses, can be of diverse color, length, width, size, pattern, imagery, or decoration. Ties can be cotton, linen, silk, polyester, microfiber, or more. The cost can vary from a couple of dollars, to $8,450 for a 24-Karat gold tie, or a quarter of a million for a diamond studded one. The designs can be traditional stripes to exuberant erotic ties, art ties (Van Gogh's Starry Nights is a popular example) or even the Ten Commandments ties. One website offers a dozen different ties of Jung, including one saying: "Your Anima is Showing."[36]

Jung spoke of the mask that we put on to confront the world, which we need in order to facilitate social relationships and interpersonal exchange. He called it the persona. Putting on a tie in the morning shows, to myself and to others, that I am leaving my personal world and entering into the realm of hierarchy, bosses, and conformity. Ties are a necessary part of the public masculine persona, the outward face of the psyche. At the same time, like a semi-permeable membrane, a tie, as part of the persona, allows a peek at what is going on inside. Within the male dress uniform, it is the one chance to let something through and reveal another side.

In my interviews about mens' experiences with ties, the most significant moment they mentioned was when they untied their ties. One man said: "The only really useful function a tie serves is the sense of relief when you get home and take it off; you feel as if you freed yourself from something, though quite what you don't know." Another added: "When I come home, I can unmask myself and return to myself." This is a daily persona ritual of millions of men: tying and untying, masking and unmasking, conforming and re-forming.

Mr. Darling, in the novel version of *Peter Pan,* illustrates "tie anxiety." Struggling to tie his tie, Mr. Darling tells his wife, "I warn you of this, mother, that unless this tie is 'round my neck we don't go out to dinner tonight, and if I don't go out to dinner tonight, I never go to the office again, and if I don't go to the office again, you and I starve, and our children will be flung in the streets."[37] For Mr. Darling, tielessness leads straight to homelessness.

Ties are an archetypal expression of persona anxiety, something everyone experiences when they worry if they are overdressed or underdressed. Dreaming about taking an exam, or forgetting their lines on stage are examples of persona anxiety. Wearing a tie is an expression of that persona anxiety, and at the same time a kind of resolution, of belonging.

One can see it every day in that big neck knot midway between a man's shoulders. Yet the question lingers for many men, "Will people take me seriously if I don't wear a tie?"[38]

Why the Buddha Remained Silent

Zen Buddhism places great value on silence: sitting in silence, walking in silence, mulling over koans in silence. There is a silent certainty that key teachings and core wisdoms can be conveyed without any explicit explanations. Words only get in the way. The origin myth of the centrality of silence lies in Buddha's famous "Flower Sermon." According to an ancient tradition, first recorded in medieval China, Gautama, the Enlightened One, gathered his disciples together for one final teaching. He stood in front of them and they sat, waiting to receive his wisdom. He said nothing. They waited. His lips did not move. Only silence, and more silence. Finally, he bent down, and from the mud of the adjacent pond, he plucked a lotus flower. Raising it just at shoulder height, he held in his hand. Nothing was spoken: only silence with the lotus. The lotus in the silence. The disciples did not comprehend. Standing alone, in front of his closest devotees, Buddha himself could not hide his own disappointment, though he said nothing. Finally, finally, one of the students, smiled. Buddha realized that this disciple alone had understood him. Buddha smiled back. In Japanese, the flower sermon, is literally "pick up flower, subtle smile" (*nengemisho*), a sort of haiku which captures this moment.

This flower sermon is about silence and certainty. How did Buddha know that his student-successor really understood what he wanted him to know? After all, the last thing he could do is to ask. More generally, how do we ever know for certain that another living soul understands us accurately when we never say a word? The ambiguity of wordless communication is exquisitely expressed in Gilbert Ryle's paradox of a man in an auditorium, winking.[39] What is the meaning of his wink? Is his closing of one eye an uncontrolled motor movement associated with his neurological disorder? Is the man giving a secret signal to a confederate? Or, is he an actor pretending to have a neurological disorder? Perhaps, he is double-signaling: pretending to his wife that his neurological disorder is worsening, while winking to a lover that their illicit rendezvous can go ahead? Seeing an eye open and close by itself does not allow us to understand the meaning of the wink. We need context. Rather amazingly, once we know the context, we usually know the wink for what it is.

In Western philosophical traditions words play such a dominant role that silence is rarely discussed. A true philosophy of silence remains to emerge in the West. Even the term "nonverbal communication" implies that words are the default form of communication. "Nonverbal" is a residual category, the "everything else." It is true that many Western icons did praise the unspoken. The great abstract expressionist painter, Mark Rothko claimed "silence is so accurate," and undoubtedly, he is correct. Paul Simon asked us to listen to "the sounds of silence," and John Cage forced us to. Herds of horses listen carefully to the silence to sense approaching danger. Disraeli argued that silence is the mother of truth. Yet, none of those lines compares to those who centered their spiritual life on wordlessness like Rumi, who said: "Let silence take you to the core of life...Live in silence." Mother Teresa proposed: "In the silence of the heart, God speaks." One feels that Buddha, sitting silently with Rumi or Mother Teresa would have felt at home.

One Western philosopher who did explore the divide between words and silence, and became one of the most influential philosophers of the twentieth century, was Ludwig Wittgenstein. He was a perfect example of the archetype of the tormented genius. Intense, original, at times overbearing, Wittgenstein demanded from others only what he insisted from himself, a relentless pursuit of clarity and truth.

He came from a most extraordinary family.[40] His father was one of the wealthiest men in the Austro-Hungarian Empire. He patronized art and music at the highest level. Gustav Mahler and Bruno Walter were household guests. The wedding present for one of Ludwig's older sisters was a full-length portrait by Gustav Klimt. Another sister was in Freud's inner circle and helped him escape to London in 1938.

There was a very dark side to the men in the Wittgenstein family. Three of Ludwig's older brothers committed suicide, at least one against a background of homosexuality. Another brother killed himself when the troops he led were routed at the end of WWI. A fourth brother, Paul, was a brilliant concert pianist who lost his right arm in the Great War. Losing an arm does not stop a Wittgenstein. Armless, he went on to have a brilliant career as a left-handed pianist, playing specially commissioned pieces by Ravel and others.

The youngest of all, Ludwig was homeschooled. He played the clarinet and could whistle entire concertos. He did original and creative work in many fields: engineering, aeronautics, mathematics, philosophy of mathematics, sculpture and architecture, besides revolutionizing modern philosophy twice. He also worked as an elementary school teacher and a gardener, and gave up his post as Professor of Philosophy at Cambridge University to work as a hospital porter during WWII. At Cambridge, he would dash out at the end of a seminar to sit in the front row of the cinema and watch cowboy movies with their simple, soothing, moral clarity.

Much of Wittgenstein's work was written when he lived alone in remote coasts of Ireland or Norway, in silence. He completed his first masterpiece while a POW at the end of WWI. That work, *Tractatus Logico-Philosophicus*, echoing Spinoza's famous title, has inspired novels, poetry, sculpture, drama, music, opera, film, video, and performance art. It ends with the famous line that draws the bold distinction between speaking and silence:

What can be said, can be said clearly. What cannot be said clearly, must be passed over in silence.[41]

There is an entire cottage industry devoted to interpreting this poetic, if cryptic phrase. He means that if you are going to speak, you must be precise and clear; if you cannot be so, then far better to keep quiet: No vague, undefined abstractions. No "waffling." Do not try to speak about that which cannot spoken.

When the book was first published, his fellow Viennese, the logical positivists, gleefully understood what cannot be said as "nonsense," which can be discarded like so much intellectual nonsense. Wittgenstein's intentions were just the opposite. Silence included the most profound aspects of human experience, such as the wonder that the world is, what Wittgenstein called the "mystical." "How can I express the importance of music in my life?" he once remarked. Perhaps the commemorative moments of silence, when we stop to remember the dead, for example, are the silences Wittgenstein was talking about. No words can adequately express the meaning of a beloved's disappearance. We may not be able to clearly and precisely say what it means, but we can point to it. Holding the lotus flower at shoulder height was the Buddha's way of pointing to what he could not say. As the Sufi mystic, Rumi, declared: silence is more eloquent than words.[42]

Silence, clearly, speaks with many voices. This multivocal aspect of silence is well expressed in a poem by the American poet, Edgar Lee Masters, author of *Spoon River Anthology*:

...There is the silence of a great hatred,
...of a great love,
...of a deep peace of mind,
...of an embittered friendship,
...of a spiritual crisis,
...of defeat.
...of those unjustly punished;
...of the dying whose hand
Suddenly grips yours.
There is the silence between father and son,
When the father cannot explain his life,
...There is the silence that comes between
husband and wife...[43]

Silence seems to contain the feeling and its opposites, so that it is not always easy to know what is not being spoken.

Psychotherapists and psychoanalysts have to be "silence experts." Through their training and with their third ear, they try to listen to the symphony of what is not being said. Some cultures (and patients) are more comfortable with silence than others. The Spanish may be the least at ease, interrupting after a second or two.

Japanese may be the most silence-rich. The Japanese dictionary lists at least twenty-one entries for what we squeeze into a single term.[44] Unlike most Westerners, Japanese are suspicious of words, and believe that silence keeps one safe, better to leave many things unsaid. Couples are characterized by what can be understood without words (*ittai*). There is a word, *ma*, for the silent interval between music notes, which expresses an entire philosophy of life. Another term, *haragei*, means literally "belly performance" in the sense of implicit mutual nonverbal understanding, so highly valued in the East. *Sasshi* refers to listener's ability to guess what a person is inferring; *ishin-denshin* a widely used for a telepathic communication; *damaru* for saying nothing in the context of speech; *chin-moku*, a spiritual practice of sinking to the bottom of the self through silence; *jakumotu*, dwelling in silence among ancestral graves; *shiginima, a* pure serene silence or *moku*, Absolute Silence. There are also many words for the negative element of silence: *mokusatsu*, to treat someone with silent contempt; *heisoku*, being cornered into silence; *shin*, prolonged silence that cuts into a conversation bringing discomfort and interrupting flow; or even a special word for the dead silence that follows a joke that falls flat. In Japan, a marriage proposal that was traditionally responded to with silence, indicated consent. Japanese expect others to understand their silence.

Because silence speaks in many shades, it is crucial for therapists to listen into the silence and only then respond appropriately. One of the most common dilemmas every therapist faces is what to do when a patient is silent or stops speaking. It is crucial for the therapist or psychoanalyst to understand the silence: Is the patient in the midst of an authentic silence, a deepening of the connection with Self? Or is this silence a psychic barrier; or is the patient drowning in their own mind. Should I respond or wait? The "to speak or not to speak" dilemma is one that therapists face every day, every hour. To offer silence is designed to provide maximum psychic space for the patient, but it can easily be felt as an abandoning: "I was drowning and you just sat there." To speak is to engage, encounter, provide support and understanding, but if mistimed, it may be perceived as intrusive, narcissistic, even annihilating: "Every time you start to speak, I disappear." Silence is especially common at the beginning of the session. The analyst's silence at the opening is designed to allow the patient to set the agenda, but the opening silence is often excruciating for certain patients, who need what Jung called a "rite d'entre," a ritual of entry into the therapeutic space. There are patients, with a dark talent for silence, who come time after time, yet remain quiet. For them, the words have been taken away from them even before they speak.

Therapists can speak in different ways. They may ask the patient what they are thinking. This standard ploy often works well when the patient tells what was going through his mind, but falls flat when the patient remains silent.[45] Then what should the therapist do? Another common approach is to provide an interpretation about the silence. A wise interpretation often opens up the well of speech, irrigating new psychic territory and deeper dialogue. But sometimes an interpretation, too, is followed by dead silence. This post-interpretation silence is difficult to comprehend. When the interpretation is spot on, the interpretation can leave patient speechless. A patient may need time to take in all the implications of a penetrating insight. In other cases, the silence may be defiant, "argumentative silence." In those cases, the patient feels so judged, misunderstood, and angry that they will not even speak. We rarely share our wounded feelings with those who have most hurt us, because, to use the contemporary Israeli phrase, we feel, "There is no one talk with." In that case of defiance, the analyst can easily misread the patient, thinking the interpretation has penetrated when it was experienced as an intrusive attack. As Elbert Hubbard once remarked: "He who does not understand your silence will probably not understand your words."[46]

Martin Buber, in his remarkable collection of autobiographical fragments, *Meetings*, gives a painful example of misreading the silence.[47] He relates an unusual morning of mystical awareness in which the veil of the surface was torn away to reveal the Beyond. Later, around noon, he received a young man, as was his custom. He listened to the young man and engaged him no less than others. But Buber failed to hear the question he did not ask. Only, later, when the young man was no longer alive, did Buber learn that the young man had not come casually, but for a decision. Ever since I read of Buber's "mismeeting," I worry. Perhaps I, too, am not hearing the questions that are not asked. I fear that I am like Buddha's disciples standing in front of the lotus but not being able to read the "visual text." My patients are holding their lotus at shoulder height and I am not smiling in comprehension.

At the end of a deep and successful analysis, there is another, special silence: when everything that needs to be said, has been said. This analysis-ending silence has the fullness of "tranquil, quiet experience of harmony"[48] or "soothing place of solace."[49] It has a fullness that is just opposite of silence as absence. Now analyst and patient may sit in a silence of togetherness, a "silence for two."

Buddha pierced the silence by plucking and raising a flower: the lotus. As in the case of Jesus and his fig, one may ask why did Buddha choose a lotus? Levi-Strauss, the notable French anthropologist who did his field work among native people of Brazil, quoted one informant as saying that some animals are good to eat, and some animals are good to think with. I think Buddha chose the lotus because it was a good flower to think with. The lotus (*Nelumbo nucifera*) is a natural symbol for consciousness. Its roots are in the mud, but its mandala-like petals lie above the surface of the muddy waters, following the sun. So, too, consciousness rises up from the earthy materialism up toward to the sunshine of enlightenment. Indian Scripture[50] compares the clear headed person unaffected by attachment, to how the lotus flower is untouched by the water below. As a result, the lotus is as embodiment of purity. Like humans, a lotus is able to regulate its own inner temperature. No matter how cold or hot the external environment, this flower can maintain inner calm, even where there is entropy all around, like a person of mindfulness. The lotus flower may be the closest thing to the eternal. A lotus seed found in an ancient, now-dry Chinese lake bed germinated and flowered after 1,300 years, tangible proof of its extraordinary resilience. Like the mind itself, all aspects of the lotus are useful, whether for food, teas, incense, aesthetics, and fabrics, but most of all as a symbol.

The lotus is the official symbol of India (and one of its main political parties). It is the logo of the Socialist Republic of Vietnam and Vietnam Airlines. Appropriately, Buddha himself is often depicted as floating on a lotus flower. The lotus, according to the Book of Symbols[51] is evocative of eros, beauty, perfection, purity, fertility, joy, resurrection, the joining of opposites, and the self-becoming. As a plant, it is visible, yet rooted in the invisible, bridging the seen and unseen. The lotus plant is the emblem of a hidden seeding place that bursts into life, like the moment of enlightenment. Not surprisingly, the lotus remains the great sign of enlightenment and spiritual kingship, as it was for the Pharaohs and Great Kings of the Ancient Near East.

The flower sermon was Buddha's way of choosing the next leader and in a way resembles the binding of Isaac, discussed in the chapter on Abraham. Passing on spiritual leadership is never simple. Consider what happened to St. Francis. He, almost single handedly, revived the spiritual vocation of the Church, seeing sun, moon, and animals as brothers and sisters. He preached the doctrine of absolute poverty, owning nothing, and eating from the Lord's Table, meaning not knowing where the next meal was coming from. It was this spiritual devotion that attracted so many followers. As the movement grew, followers asked if it were possible to own a prayer book. Francis was adamant in his refusal: "First you want a book, then you will ask for a chair, then a table and next a house for when it rains and so on until the message of poverty will be perverted." But his own disciples did not listen to him. They obtained books, then chairs, then tables and finally libraries and monasteries. Franciscan monks, although taking the oath of poverty personally, belong to one of the wealthiest monastic orders in the world.

Returning to our theme of wordlessness: What can one say about silence? The most precise answer is that silence allows for semantically creative breadth that words can never have. Being together in silence can be both the most agonizing and most unifying experience that humans ever have.

Why Did Jonah Sit in the Shade?

Jonah is a man with a special gift. When he speaks, entire cities reflect on their misdeeds and return to the Way. He is the maestro of moral change and the rock star of repentance. But Jonah has a problem, an ego problem. His pitch is as a prophet of doom: "Unless you change, your city shall be destroyed." When people listen and "return" (as repentance is called in Hebrew), God shows compassion, forgives, and spares the city. A compassionate man of God would be thrilled. But not Jonah. How does Jonah react? He is angry, disappointed, and even suicidal. Rather than compassionate concern, he is worried only about his reputation. He is anxious that the next time he cries out that devastation is near, the people will not believe him. Jonah is afraid of becoming the prophet who cried wolf.

In terms of Erich Neumann's theory of the ego-Self axis, a prophet must allow for the vision of the Divine to flow unimpeded from the Self through the ego and into the consciousness of the collective. Greek seers would enter into a dissociated state in order to prophesy, like the sibyl at the famous oracle at Delphi. Such trance dissociation lent authenticity and legitimacy to her utterances. Trance shows that it is the gods who are speaking, and not the prophetess herself. Biblical prophecy is very different. The ego remains intact and so the individual seer must remain "clean" of personal projections in order to serve as a pure conduit for the Self. As a result, Biblical prophets can never desire to be prophets. Even when chosen, these seers resist their calling. Moses fills an entire chapter with reasons why he is **not** the right man for the job. Jeremiah protests, "I do not know how to speak: I am only a child!"[52] Their very resistance to the role lends authenticity. It is not Moses or Jeremiah speaking, but rather a Divine Voice speaking through them. Jonah as a prophet is a servant of the Self, calling people back to the Right Way. However, his ego concerns for his persona ("what will people think of me") get in the way. Jonah, therefore, suffers from primary disturbance in his ego-Self axis.

The Book of Jonah begins with God telling Jonah to travel and warn the inhabitants of the great city of Nineveh. He knows it is his destiny to go and speak the warning. Instead, he decides to flee to Tarshish, at the other end of the Mediterranean Sea. The ensuing voyage of Jonah then becomes a metaphor for mental disturbance. The waters, symbol of the unconscious, become stirred up and stormy. Jonah falls asleep in the depth of the ship, indicative of his profound state of unawareness of the danger he is in. When he does realize he is the cause of the storm, he asks to be cast into the sea, symbolically, thrown into the depth of the un-conscious where is swallowed by a great fish, a devouring complex. Inside the unconscious, he re-establishes ego-Self axis and reconnects with the Lord: "Out of my distress I cried to Yahweh and He answered me..."[53]

Reborn, Jonah is cast upon the shore, and is given a second chance. This time he does accept his destiny and travels to the metropolis of Nineveh. Again, he is magically able to speak directly to the hearts and superegos of the people. The people, and then their King, respond dramatically. They fast, put on sackcloth, sit in ashes and beg for mercy, saying "...let everyone renounce his evil ways and violent behavior. Who knows? Perhaps God will change his mind and relent and renounce his burning wrath, so that we shall not perish."[54] God sees their genuine turning away from evil behaviors and forgives them. This is where the book of Jonah should end, as a paradigm of possibility of profound change and divine forgiveness. It is because of this that the book of Jonah is read aloud in synagogues on the afternoon of the most solemn day in the Hebrew calendar, Yom Kippur. But the book does not end there. In the fourth and last chapter, there is a strange coda.

After giving his pitch, Jonah leaves the city. He finds a vantage point to the east of the city and waits to see what will happen. Does Jonah rejoice that his words were so effective? On the contrary, Jonah, furious and distressed, wants to die, saying, "That was why I first tried to flee to Tarshish, since I knew you were a tender, compassionate God, slow to anger, rich in faithful love, who relents about inflicting disaster. So now, Yahweh, please take my life, for I might as well be dead as go on living."[55] Jonah builds a temporary structure, called a "sukkah." It is the same word used for what Jews dwell in during the eponymous, fall festival. The contrast between festive joyfulness of *sukkot* and Jonah's lonely torment in his *sukka* is almost unbearable.

It is as if Jonah has learned nothing from his aquatic experience under the water, inside the great fish. Jonah resembles those individuals in analysis who make a dramatic breakthrough, a true "ah-ha" experience. But at the next session, they behave as if nothing had happened. They may even ask, "What did we talk about last time?" Instead of transformation, there is a "regressive restoration of the persona." Jung used that term to describe individuals who undergo an intense, psychotic episode whose hidden purpose is to expand the structure of the psyche. Instead of using the psychotic break as an opportunity for the psyche to develop, their only wish is to return to what they were previously. As a result, they become a caricature of their former selves. Jonah, who had experienced the power of the dialogue with the Self ("I cried to You and You answered me.") is re-possessed by an egotistical, persona complex.

In the Bible, as in therapy, nothing happens by chance. Jonah chooses to walk off toward the east. Within the symbolic geography of the bible, going east clearly echoes the direction into which Cain wandered. The language of Jonah's anguish is a clear echo to Cain's distress. Although Jonah has not actually killed anyone, he wants the population of an entire city to die, just because he said it would. Mass destruction fantasies are not uncommon during psychotic experiences. "My thoughts are destroying an entire city" or "I am worse than Hitler" may be heard as people struggle to come to terms with their own inner destructiveness. Perhaps this perspective helps understand the meaning of Jonah sitting in the shade, trapped beneath the penumbra of what Jung called the shadow. To reconnect with himself, Jonah needs to learn about his own shadow. God has forgiven the people of Nineveh. Will He forgive Jonah? God wants to teach Jonah a lesson, and one he won't forget this time. Like a positive trickster, God prepares a psychological manipulation in service of a higher purpose. In the broiling sun, he prepares a *"kikayon."* The Hebrew word, *kikayon,* appears only once in the entire Hebrew Bible. Such words are called *hapax legomenon* by scholars, and their meaning necessarily remains obscure. From the context, it seems a quick growing, broad leaf shade tree. It is usually translated as "castor oil plant," which is what *kikayon* means in modern Hebrew. In any case, Jonah was delighted with the tree-like plant that provided soothing shade.

Now God sets His plan to work. A worm attacks the plant, which then withers and dies. A brutal east wind bears down on Jonah so hard that he is overcome. Like a good psychoanalyst, God tries to get Jonah to reflect on his own feelings: "Are you right to be angry about the castor-oil plant?"[56] Jonah replies, to the reader's horror, "I'm so angry I wish I were dead." God's response to Jonah's suicidal, self-absorption sounds like an attempt to give Jonah perspective: "You are concerned about the castor oil plant, for which you have not labored and which you did not rear, which came up in a night, and perished in a night; and should I not be concerned for Nineveh, that great city, in which are more than one hundred and twenty thousand persons that cannot discern between your right hand and their left hand; and also much cattle?"[57]

If we look at the scene symbolically, then we can understand shade and sun represent two psychological states; the light of consciousness and the darkness of the shadow. For Jonah, the intensity of self-awareness was unbearable, symbolized by the sun bearing down on him. Jonah took refuge and delight in the shadow of moral blindness. Now one can understand God's intention, like that of a good psychoanalyst of moving Jonah from the darkness of self-deception to illumination of moral awareness.

The confrontation between God and Jonah recalls a similar, dramatic encounter between God and Job. Toward the end of that book, God speaks angrily to Job out of the whirlwind: "Where were you when I founded the earth?...Let him who wants to correct God give an answer!" Job replies: "I am too ashamed; I have nothing to say... I know that you can do everything... I detest [myself] and repent in dust and ashes."[58]

No one knows what to make of this encounter. Jung gave his intriguing answer in *Answer to Job*: the ego must suffer to change the Self. The text portrays a man's experience of an overwhelming encounter with the Self. Job's ego is put into its puny place. Yet, as discussed in the chapter on Job, there is evidence that his suffering did lead him to understanding the suffering of others and then act compassionately in a new and radical way.

God wants to teach Jonah compassion. He wants Jonah to understand that the citizens of Nineveh are real people who deserve compassion. Jonah has saved an entire city, but he does not understand the simple meaning of being his brother's keeper. Jonah is someone who can bring others to a *tikkun,* but in his blindness, is unable to repair himself. His attitude recalls gifted therapists who are genuinely able to help others, but whose own personal lives are in shambles.

Teaching compassion is not easy, since it involves a shift away from the ego toward the Self. Nevertheless, there are techniques for teaching compassion. One approach is to stimulate the imagination to feel for the "other" by putting themselves in their shoes or wheelchairs. How does a disabled person feel when they cannot climb the stairs to a toilet and soil themselves in their wheelchair? How does a sexually abused adolescent feel when the place they most fear is their own home? A different approach is teaching through example. Dalai

Lama teaches that if you want to be happy, make others happy by practicing compassion. If you want someone to be compassionate, practice compassion toward them. According to the Tibetan leader, compassion is highly infectious.

In trying to teach compassion, God leaves Jonah to broil in the burning sun. Then, He gives Jonah some soothing shade that He then, abruptly, takes away. Angry parents often apply this technique when trying to discipline an envy-full child. A child grabs a brother's toys, not because he wants to play with it, but because he cannot stand his brother playing with it. The parent confiscates the child's own favorite toy, saying, "Now you will see what it feels like!" with decidedly mixed results at best. Some children really understand how their brother feels and become their keeper. Others just wait for the parent to be out of sight to clobber his brother or destroy the toy. For them, the sin is getting caught.

I have always found the abruptness of the ending of the book of Jonah ("and also much cattle?") very disturbing. Some scholars claim that the point of the abrupt ending of the Book of Jonah is the point: to give the reader the experience of incompleteness. The Bible views history as an ongoing dialogue between God and man. Man searching for God; God in search of Man, to use Heschel's telling phrase.[59] Yet, it is a dialogue that can be severed. Joseph Heller's inspired retelling of the story of David after the death of his son, Absalom, gives an evocative account of just such a break:

In solitude, I was raging at the Lord,
seething with scornful
belligerence toward the Lord, and spoiling
for a fight with
Him. I really could not keep my temper.

David continues:

I wanted to have it out
with Him, I was ready to curse God and
die. But He would not
take me on. . . .

David receives a most unexpected
response:

I received instead the answer I least
expected.
Silence.
It is the only answer I have gotten from
Him since.[60]

Jonah felt compassion for a shade plant but not for an entire city. I believe the Book's ending is like an analyst's interpretation that leaves the patient speechless. But it also emphasizes that if one behaves as badly as Jonah does, then the dialogue between man and God will break off and God, being God, will always have the last word.

Jonah's stunned silence resembles that universal experience of having a dream that suddenly stops. How can one ever know the rest of a dream? One technique that Jung pioneered was "completing the dream." Jung claimed that dreams, like the classical Greek drama, typically had four distinctive phases that Aristotle described: introduction, development, and then a crisis, followed by the *lysis* or culmination. Most dreams cease in the crisis phase; nightmares always do. Jung felt continuing the dream via active imagination can be revealing and healing. I invite the reader to reflect and continue the Book of Jonah. If the Book of Jonah had continued, what do you imagine would happen?

Why Jesus Cursed a Fig Tree

Jesus is walking with his disciples to Jerusalem for the very last time. In the distance, suddenly he sees a fig tree. He develops a keen desire to eat of its fruit. As he approaches the fruit tree, he discovers that although the tree is full of leaves, it has no fruit. Abruptly, He curses the tree saying, "May no one ever eat fruit from you again"[61] or "May you never bear fruit again."[62] Immediately, or the next day, depending on the Gospel, the tree withers. The Talmud claimed that when a fruit tree is deliberately destroyed, its cry can be heard round the world.[63] The death of a fruit tree in Jesus' time would be considered a catastrophic event.

What is surprising is not that Jesus, the prophet of love curses the innocent if disappointing, fruit tree. Jesus can certainly talk tough as when he speaks to his mother and sister:

> "Do not suppose that I have come to bring peace to the earth. I did not come to bring peace, but a sword. For I have come to 'set a man against his father, a daughter against her mother, and a

daughter-in-law against her mother-in-law'; and 'a man's enemies *will be* those of his *own* household."[64]

No. What is astonishing is that Jesus seems to have forgotten that figs do not ripen in the early spring in the holy land. Jesus expects something that he must have known was unavailable. Jesus is yearning for fruit out of season. Why does Jesus want the impossible? Why does Jesus curse the fig tree?

Perhaps, in one sense, we all want the impossible: To have our desires filled immediately and unconditionally; to have people know what we want without having to ask for it; to feel omnipotent and have the power to get exactly what we want, exactly when we want it. Since these are the normal wishes of babies, Jesus's relation to the fig may be illuminated by the way in which psychoanalysts conceptualize how babies deal with contradictory demands of love, desire, and destructiveness. Donald W. Winnicott, in one of his most famous articles, "The Use of An Object," wrote that what the child wants is to tell the mother, "I destroyed you." Surviving the child's aggression allows a new and more mature relation to unfold because the mother is outside his omnipotent control. Winnicott explains:

From now on the subject [the child] says: 'Hello object!' 'I destroyed you.' 'I love you.' 'You have value for me because of your survival of my destruction of you.' 'While I am loving you I am all the time destroying you in (unconscious) *fantasy.* Here fantasy begins for the individual.[65]

For Jesus, the opposite is true. The fig tree, the object of his desire, does not survive his destructiveness; nor does it exist outside omnipotent control. This is all the more surprising, since Jesus at the beginning of his vocaton did renounce such magical omnipotence. At the very beginning of his spiritual career, Jesus was tested by Satan. But the Son of God refused to turn stones into bread, to jump off from a height, or to rule the world. Jesus wisely rejected the grandiose feeling that he could do anything, even the impossible.

Another way to understand why Jesus cursed the fig tree has to do with the nature of love and hate. Ordinarily, love and hate are seen as primary opposites. Psychoanalysts, however, believe that hate and love are actually close together. Both involve intense investment of libido, differentiated only by a simple positive or negative sign, as "dislike" is a variant on "like." Indeed, words may mean the thing and its opposite, as in the Book of Job, when the same Hebrew word means both to bless God and to curse God. It also explains why a hateful quarrel may end in loving embrace, as hate turns back into love. Indifference is another kind of opposite of love, in which emotional meter is switched to zero. One of Jung's most brilliant insights is his claim that the true opposite of love is neither hate nor indifference, but power: "When loves rules, there is no will to power; and where power predominates, there love is lacking. One is the shadow of the other."[66] According to Jung, genuine loving never involves trying to force yourself or your feelings on a beloved; if you are doing so, then it is not love. It is power pretending to be love.

The theme of the impossible is highlighted in Jesus' subsequent comment to the disciples when he learns that the fig tree has withered. Here are Jesus remarks as recorded in the fuller version in the Gospel of Mark[67]:

> Truly, I tell you, if anyone says to this mountain, 'Go, throw yourself into the sea,' and does not doubt in their heart but believes that what they say will happen, it will be done for them. Therefore I tell you, whatever you ask for in prayer, believe that you have received it, and it will be yours.[68]

The context of Jesus' remarks seems all the more puzzling. After all, it was Jesus himself who asked for a fruit He did not receive. Moreover, his promise: *whatever you ask for in prayer, believe that you have received it, and it will be yours,* cannot be literally true. So many people have prayed and believed.

Although Jesus remarks have doctrinal and theological importance, I can only focus only on their significance for the psychology of the impossible. Jesus seems to be saying "nothing is impossible." Mountains can throw themselves into the sea; asking that a prayer will be answered will make it come true. Believing the impossible will make the impossible come true. Clearly, Jesus seems to be saying do not stop believing in the impossible. Great leaders have always valued the impossible. Nelson Mandela said, "It always seems impossible until it's done."[69] Theodore Roethke added, "What we need is more people who specialize in the impossible." The Red Queen in Wonderland believed as many as six impossible things before breakfast. I wonder if Jesus felt like Caligula in Albert Camus' eponymous play, who says, "I suddenly felt a desire for the impossible... The world as it is, is unbearable. That's why I need the moon, or happiness, or immortality, or something that may sound insane, but would help correct this world."[70] Clinical work occasionally deals with the "impossible love complex": women who fall in love with unattainable men; men who cannot commit because they are pursuing an ever-elusive, anima instead of a spouse. In those cases, the therapist becomes, "Love's Executioner," to use Irving Yalom's memorable phrase. The therapist needs to draw them away from their quest for the impossible and back into life.

Nevertheless, the limits of the impossible are no longer clear. Flying to the moon, swapping genders or organs, speaking simultaneously to people in a dozen different countries were all impossible, until recently. In this sense, Jesus is right in saying that the limits of the impossible are not fixed. What we think is impossible today, may well be doable tomorrow.

Perhaps the question is better asked, why did Jesus want a fig, in the first place, and not a date or pomegranate. In the Bible, figs were strongly associated with peace and prosperity. Scripture uses figs as symbolic indicators of the good life in the good land, as when the prophet presents an ideal time, *"where every man will sit under his own vine and under his own fig tree..."[71]* In contrast, Jeremiah describes God's wrath in terms of the absence of figs: *"There will be no figs on the tree, and their leaves will wither. What I have given them, will be taken from them."[72]* Jesus echoes and plays off Jeremiah when He says, *"He who has not, it shall be taken away."[73]*

The erotic quality of fresh figs is well known. The Rabbis compared the stages of sexual awakening in the female to the growth of the fig: "The sages spoke of a woman in a parable: an unripe fig, a fig in its early ripening stage and a ripe fig. An unripe fig: while she is yet a child; A fig in its early ripening stage: when she is in her youth... A ripe fig—as soon as she becomes of majority age, her father has no longer any right over her."[74] One might add: a dried-up fig is like a woman post menopause. The fig tree has been called the tree of many breasts, since like the Great Mother, the more fruit one gathers, the more one discovers. Plutarch said the fruit resembled male sexual organs. The fig with its fruit was sacred to Dionysus and Priapus, him of the eternal erection. It is for them, the true fruit of passion. The

Bodhi tree (*ficus religiosa*) under which Buddha received enlightenment was also a fig.

Jesus would surely have known the ancient Hebrew tradition that claimed the fruit in the Garden of Eden was a fig.[75] Genesis seems deliberately to not state the specific fruit of the tree of the knowledge of good and evil. But it does state that Adam and Eve used fig leaves to cover their body. Working from internal evidence alone, figs are the prime suspects as the first fruit of temptation. Identifying the fruit as fig adds depth to the story. The fig that caused shame covered shame.

Jesus' cursing the fig tree is striking deviation from his main message of overcoming aggression, loving your enemy and turning the other cheek. Indeed, the conclusion of Jesus' sermon after learning of the death of the fig tree is one of his most powerful statements: "*And when you stand praying, if you hold anything against anyone, forgive them, so that your Father in heaven may forgive you your sins...*"[76] This key psychological insight is that forgiving others is the royal road to being forgiven. Christianity and Judaism as sister religions share much, but they differ significantly in their attitude toward forgiveness. In Christianity, forgiveness is fundamental. One cannot be a believer without acknowledging the necessity and power of forgiveness. But the process of forgiveness is essentially an internal one. I recall an interview with a black South African mother, whose son was brutally murdered by police during the time of apartheid. She was asked whether she forgave her son's killer. Immediately, she replied, "Of course, I forgive him. Otherwise, how will Jesus forgive me my sins." The bereft mother never came face-to-face with her son's murderer, yet she can forgive him since the site of the forgiveness is in the mother's soul.

In Judaism, such "internal forgiveness" does not exist. A person must sincerely regret his action but that is not enough. They must come to the person who they hurt and then ask for forgiveness. And even then, there is no religious obligation to forgive. For Jews, the space for forgiveness is not internal but in the interpersonal, in the "between." Indeed, the Hebrew tradition makes a sharp distinction between two sorts of sins: those between a person and his "fellow," to use the Hebrew phrase (literally "Adam and his friend"), and those between a person and the Divine, which the Jew in this context, calls, *hamakom*, literally, "The Place." The Day of Atonement deals only with violations of divine commandments. It cannot help with sins against other people. Sins against fellow humans cannot be forgiven, even by God Himself.

In my clinical work, I do meet decent people with hypercritical, hateful feelings toward themselves. The conventional wisdom is that these ever-present feelings are introjections of a mother's or father's unloving emotional attitude toward them at critical periods in their childhood. A child in that situation is faced with a question: Who is to blame? A young child thinks only in the "either/or" style of splitting: either it is my parents' fault, or it is my own fault. If it is the parent's fault, then the child is doomed. The child is trapped forever in a loveless situation. If it is the child's own fault, then if they can become a better, more perfect child, then perhaps, just perhaps, the love from the parent may be restored. Developing a punishing superego is the wise choice, but it comes with an enormous inner price. Unlike most people, they treat others much better than they treat themselves. They dare not love their neighbors like themselves; instead they treat their neighbors much better than they treat themselves. They are unable to forgive or feel compassion toward themselves. The anger they could not feel toward the all-powerful parent is turned back inside themselves.

Forgiveness is not only the concern of religions, but something central to the therapeutic process. In analysis, people need to find a way to forgive themselves and the people who hurt them. Psychological treatment usually follows a "Christian" orientation of allowing compassion to enter into an inner world filled with hate and accusation. Sometimes, the work needs to be more "Jewish" in seeking a repair in the "in between," between the person who was injured and the one who injured.

From a psychological point of view, Jesus said that the royal road to forgiving ourselves, is a loving, forgiving attitude toward those who sinned against us. By loving one's parent-enemy and turning the other cheek, a person can remove the source of inner judgment/hate and eventually feel the divine-like forgiveness of a new start. Yet, how did Jesus the man feel when he saw the results of his curse, that his wishes had destroyed a living tree? I think when he learned that the fig had withered, he understood what it means to commit a destructive act. It is Jesus at his most human. At that moment, he realized the impact of destructive aggression and truly understood what it meant to forgive.

Why Job Became
the First Feminist

In the opening, frame story of the Book of Job, there is a description of Job's children. [77] His seven sons and three daughters seem an ideal sibling group. Taking turns, the brothers feast at each other's house, inviting their three sisters to join them. Job, in sharp contrast to his celebrating, carefree children, is a very anxious parent, "for Job thought, perhaps my children have sinned and blasphemed God in their thoughts."[78] Job might well qualify for a psychiatric diagnosis of anxiety disorder, with obsessional guilty thoughts. Strangely, no reason is given for why Job feels so responsible for the sinful thoughts of his children. There is no obvious clue concerning the cause of Job's anxiety in the text. Job makes special, expiation sacrifices for the imagined sins of his sons and daughters. Job's anxiety is an interesting overture to the dialogues that follow. It is very possible that Job projected his own unconscious doubt onto his children, leaving him consciously devout and pure in his belief. Job, in the rest of the Book, never doubts that he is without sin, and despite urgings of his wife, never curses at God. Significantly, this absolute certainty of his innocence, led Rabbis to claim that Job was not a Jew. A Jew will always have lingering doubt about oneself and can never be sure he or she is free from sin. Job never says **perhaps** I have sinned and blasphemed God in my thoughts. Yet, Job's worst fears do come true, like self-fulfilling prophecy. All ten children are killed while feasting at their eldest brother's house.

One of the important questions Jung asked in *Answer to Job* concerned the meaning of Job's sufferings. Was Job changed by his suffering? Was God? A close reading of the final passages reveals that Job was indeed transformed, but in an unexpected way. Toward the end of the Book of Job, there is a sudden and unexpected appearance of Job's own brothers and sisters who "consoled and comforted him for all the misfortune that the Lord had brought upon him..."[79] Job's brothers and sisters (did we even know he had brothers and sisters?) arrive and acting as ritual siblings, are uniquely able to comfort and console. Job's brothers and sisters are able to do what his four "friends" failed at miserably.[80]

The siblings eat all together and give Job ceremonial mourning gifts, restoring a sense of community Job had lost in the depth of his grief. Reminiscent of holocaust survivors who lost and recreated their murdered families, Job has 10 more children born to him. Once again, he has seven sons and three daughters. What has changed? No change is recorded in connection with his sons. But a dramatic change occurs in his relationship to his daughters. Previously, his daughters were nameless. Now each daughter is given a warm and special individual name: Jemimah, Keziah, Keren-happuch. These personal names emphasize their individuality and Job's individuated relationship with each one of them. They are praised for their beauty: "Throughout the land there were no woman as beautiful as the daughter of Job."[81] I understand this phrase as reflecting how their father now perceived his daughters. Most significantly, they are given inheritance rights equal to their brothers. Job changes the patriarchal system of inheritance and treats his daughters as full and equal.

In an inner way, Job's suffering seems to have changed his relationship to his inner feminine. I can now offer an interpretation of Job's anxiety at the beginning of the story. Previously, Job, I suggest, unconsciously experienced his daughters' resentment at being dependent on their brothers, as Joseph's brothers were.[82] His anxiety was the result of his subtly picking up some of the unconscious feelings of his children, as an analyst does with a patient using what Michael Fordham called, "syntonic countertransference" or by Melanie Klein, "projective identification."

These sisters had no right to openly complain, and indeed may not have been fully aware of their own feelings. Living by the rules of patriarchal society, the sisters had received "generous," if patronizing treatment by their brothers. Nevertheless, one cannot deny the fundamental unfairness of such gender-discrimination they must have felt in their hearts. The anxiety Job was feeling at the beginning of the Book was in this view a reflection of his daughters' unexpressed conflict. On the one hand, there was resentment and on the other hand, there was gratitude. If this reading is plausible, then Job's action to give estates to his daughters is a revolutionary act of repair or "tikkun." It resolves a secret envy among the siblings, closing the circle of envy that began with Cain. Job was a pioneering feminist. Out of his own suffering, he learned compassion for the dispossessed. Perhaps that is the hidden meaning of the phrase, "Thus the Lord blessed the latter years of Job's life more than the former."[83] Job's suffering transformed him from an anxious father into the first feminist.

Why Abraham Agreed to Kill

Imagine that you are a child again, playing happily. Suddenly, the door opens and your father appears. He says you are going on a journey together. Walking for a long time in silence together, you wonder where you are going. Finally, you gather your courage and ask your father, "Where are we going?" Your father replies: "We will know when we get there." You continue climbing together up the hillside. When you reach the top, father pushes you down against a rock, pulls out a dagger and raises his arm… You wake up from a nightmare.[84]

This nightmare is inspired by a terrible story of the sacrifice of Isaac, known in Hebrew as the *akeda*, "the binding of Isaac."[85] Abraham, who has yearned for a son, is told to offer his son up as a sacrifice. He takes him on a journey to Mt. Moriah, traditionally identified as the Temple Mount of Jerusalem, where he binds him and raises his dagger. He is stopped only at the last minute by an "angel-messenger" (the Hebrew word, *malach,* can mean either), who actually has to call out twice. When first considering the *akeda*, a father deliberately planning to murder his son, it seems like the act of a madman. Yet Jewish, Christian and Moslem traditions all herald it as a supreme moment of faith.[86] Nevertheless, Abraham seems more of a psychiatric case: a psychotic, psychopathic, senex personality, suffering from command hallucinations, possessed by a grandiose "God complex." It seems a horrible, religious perversion.

Abraham[87] is often understood as Knight of Faith and the Prince of Obedience. God the Father tells Abraham, to kill the son he loves and Abraham obeys with fear and trembling. The Supreme Divine Authority demands obedience, or in Jungian terms, an all-powerful Self dictates to an overpowered, submissive ego. Most interpretations of the *akeda,* from Kierkegaard to Bob Dylan, are based on this view, well illustrated in the opening lyrics of Bob Dylan's song, "Highway 61 Revisited"[88]:

> Oh God said to Abraham, "Kill me a son."
> Abe says, "Man, you must be puttin' me on."

The lyrics continue:

> God say, "No." Abe say, "What?"

And build to the crescendo:

God say, "You can do what you want Abe,
but
The next time you see me comin' you
better run."

But this interpretation has a serious flaw. It is based on a mistranslation of the Biblical Hebrew. In most English translations, God says to Abraham, "Take your son." But the Hebrew does not say, "Take." The Hebrew phrase is: "*kakh na.*" "Take" would involve "*kakh*" alone; so, what is "*na*" doing there? "*na*" is an untranslatable term indicating a polite request. The Hebrew might be better translated as "Please take." or "Will you take?" but certainly **not** the command, "Take!"

In Genesis alone, there are 25 examples of "*na.*" Each one is a request, even an unusual request as when Abram asks his wife to pretend to be his sister; or when God asks Abraham to look up and count the stars in the night sky. Whatever *akeda* is, it is not about an Abraham possessed by authoritarian great father complex demanding submission. Rather, Abraham is asked to make a choice. To choose between two things that he loves best.

I am a passionate Jew, but when I read the *akeda*, I wish I were a Christian. For a Christian believer, the "sacrifice of Isaac" makes sense. It is the clearest pre-figuration of the sacrifice of a Son by another Father. The parallels between Isaac and Jesus are striking. Like Isaac, Jesus is His Father's beloved son; like Isaac, Jesus travels to receive his fate in Jerusalem; like Isaac, Jesus carries wood on his back up a mountainside; like Isaac, Jesus asks one poignant question of his Father. There is, however, one crucial difference, between the Old Testament and the New. Isaac is saved at the very last minute, while Jesus, the archetypal abandoned son, dies alone on the cross, crying out: "Father, Father, why have you abandoned me?"[89] The prophet of Love encounters *thanatos*; while Isaac returns from his near death experience with a new ability to love, as is revealed in his new ability to love his new wife, Rebecca.[90] For Jesus, death is a prelude to resurrection; for Isaac, it is the beginning of his initiation as a man who has experienced Divine Presence.

Jung taught that people are often unconsciously trapped in a myth. Understanding the myth may set the psyche free. From this mythological perspective, Abraham is enmeshed in a "Laius complex." Laius was Oedipus' father and arguably embodied the archetype of the terrible father. Laius heard an oracle predicting that his own son was destined to murder him. In fear of his unborn murderer, Laius refused to be fruitful and multiply. His wife, Jocasta, following the example of Abraham's nieces (who are discussed in the next chapter "Why did Lot's Wife Look Back?"), made him drunk and stole his semen. Soon she was pregnant. When the child was born, Laius demanded that the terrifyingly, threatening baby be murdered. A rod was rammed through his child's foot and this is the origin of his name,

Oedi-pus, meaning "swollen foot." It was his mother, Jocasta, who actually turned over her baby to die slowly of starvation on a Theban hillside—a fact that Freud, who had a highly idealized view of mother-son relationships, ignored. As a result, Freud "misread" the Oedipal story, as a story starting with seduction rather than child abuse. Had Freud paid attention to the beginning of the Oedipus myth, he might have seen that parents' impulse to kill their child is a universal, archetypal situation, that we can all recognize when a parent exclaims, "If you do that, I'll kill you."

Laius complex, an archetypal aspect of the negative Great Father, is well illustrated in the first generations of Greek mythology. Cronus envied the power of his father, Uranus, the ruler of the universe. With the help of his mother, Gaia, Cronus attacked his father, cutting off his genitals with a sickle, and casting the severed phallus into the sea. Cronus became the absolute ruler and at first, his reign was a Golden Age. Cronus learned from his own experience that his own offspring would overcome him. He devoured his own children as soon as they were born. Cronus is not alone. A similar Laius situation is found in the opening of the Book of Exodus, when Pharaoh demands the midwives kill all Hebrew male babies at birth. Herod's massacre of the innocents recorded in the Gospels[91] is another example of a Great Father possessed by a Laius complex. These fathers want to defeat time and live forever; they are self-absorbed narcissists who fear their own generativity. To allow your son to live is to accept that one day you will die and your son will continue after you. That is the hidden link of sex and death. The first task of a son is to survive his father's murderous envy.

Collectively, the Laius complex expresses a cultural complex involving the psychological power struggle between the generations. Laius, now an old man, "unconsciously" meets his son whom he refuses to recognize. Neither son nor father is willing to give way and let the other pass. This stalemate represents an archetypal conflict between the old and younger generations. The older generation, symbolized by Laius, is blocking the way of the younger to inherit their power and status. Laius acts out a murderous envy of the younger generation's vitality and youthfulness. Political revolutionaries often develop a Laius complex once they are in power. Once entrenched, they may become an aging senex, never relinquishing their position of power. They view younger comrades all as disloyal traitors coming to displace them. Stalin and his purges, Mao and his Cultural Revolution and the once revolutionary regimes of Cuba or Vietnam, whose average age of the leadership is eighty, all fall under the psychology of a Laius Complex.

Just as in the Book of Job, the text of Genesis places the *akeda* narrative within a frame: "Now after these events. God tested Abraham." The first phrase, "After these events," I believe, holds the key to the meaning of the *akeda*. It demands that *akeda,* be viewed, not as an isolated act, but within the context of a developmental sequence. Every time this phrase, "Now after these events," appears in Scripture, it refers to preceding events, often in the previous chapter. The previous chapter, however, provides little hint of a context. Abraham reaches a pinnacle of paternity, status, and success. The miracle child Isaac, whose name means "laughter/laughing" is born. A local king, Abimelech (literally, My Father, the King) comes to make a treaty of everlasting friendship, saying, "God is with you in all things"; Abraham calls out "the name of the Lord, the everlasting God." These events describe what Daniel Levinson, author of *The Seasons of a Man's Life*, called a "stable period."[92] Stable periods are times of consolidation and mature achievement, unlike periods of turmoil and transition like a midlife crisis. There is, however, one traumatic event that puts *akeda* into a father-son perspective, and it concerns his relation to his first-born son, Ishmael, whose name means: "God will hear/hears."

Shortly after the miracle child Isaac is weaned, Abraham's wife, Sarah, demands that Abraham expel their adopted, surrogate son, saying, "Drive out this slave woman and her son, for the son of this slave-woman shall not share inheritance with my son, with Isaac!" Alice Miller, author of *The Drama of the Gifted Child*[93] calls Abraham, the "archetypal child abuser." Abraham is in a moral quandary, torn between his loyalty to his wife and his duty as a father. The text says clearly: "The matter was exceedingly bad in Abraham's eyes because of his son."[94] A contemporary parallel might be a blended family in which a new wife demands that her husband send her multiracial, adopted step-son off to a military academy to "make a man out of him". In reality, her goal is to get him out of the way and leave the inheritance clear for her own biological child. Evolutionary psychology explains the logic of these selfish actions. Just as a lion who takes over a new pride will kill the cubs of his predecessor, so too, a new wife, may symbolically try to do the same.

The moral conflict that Abraham undergoes is not elaborated, but its silent impact is strong. When a divine prophecy urges him "to follow Sarah in all things," he sends Ishmael and his mother into the desert to an almost certain death. Why does Abraham, with his exquisite moral sensibilities, do what he knows to be wrong? In the dynamics of psychology, Abraham is obeying his Inner Voice. The language of the revelation, "Follow Sarah in all things she says!"[95] may indicate a powerful need to honor the feminine voice. The fate of Ishmael and Isaac are linked: Like Isaac, Abraham sends his first, beloved son off to the most bitter of fates. Like Isaac, Ishmael sets out in the early morning—leading to suggestions that God appeared to Abraham in a dream— or even that the entire *akeda* is a dream; like Isaac, Ishmael would be dead, except for the intervention of an angel/messenger. Ishmael's sacrifice prefigures and parallels *akeda*. In a sense, it is the first *akeda*! It suggests a lingering, unresolved Laius orientation of Abraham toward his sons.

Sarah's possessive power complex toward Isaac would have led to excessive closeness between mother and son, or even, a pathological maternal symbiosis. Breaking such symbiosis is not simple. Jung noted that fear of the father may drive a boy out of his identification with his mother, or it may cause him to cling still more, leading to a neurotic situation. Abraham's Inner Voice may well have understood the need to dramatically sever this regressive mother-son bond. A fascinating piece of cross-cultural research in Africa discovered that the greater the maternal symbiosis, for example, as measured by mother-son sleeping arrangements, the more brutal were male initiation rituals.[96] From that perspective, the *akeda* was just such a traumatic, male initiation rite, separating Isaac from his mother and from the maternal. Not surprisingly, Jewish tradition links Sarah's death with the fatal effect of her hearing about the *akeda*.

The next phrase in the text of Genesis 22, "God tested Abraham," creates a tension between the reader and Abraham. We know it is a test; Abraham does not. The reader, participating in the scene, longs to warn Isaac, "Your father is going to kill you!" As a result, the reader becomes a complicit participant in the unfolding divine psychodrama.

God tells Abraham to take his son and "offer him up there as an offering—up upon one of the mountains."[97] How does Abraham respond? Does he protest and cry against this terrible injustice? No, he remains silent. To help us understand Abraham's silence, it is important to examine one previous encounter with his Voice. In Chapter 18, Abraham learns from God that He is about to annihilate the wicked cities of the Plain, which we remember as Sodom and Gomorrah. Abraham responds with unparalleled intimacy and dialogue:

> Abraham came close and said:
> Will you really sweep away the innocent
> along with the guilty?
> Perhaps there are fifty innocent within
> the city,
> Will you really sweep it away?
> …Heaven forbid for you!
> The judge of all earth – will not do what
> is just?[98]

In this dynamic encounter between ego and Self, one can see the essence of Abraham's spiritual revolution: humanity's relationship with Divinity is based **not** on blind submission to a higher authority, but on dialogue and universal values. While a man must know his place— Abraham says, "I am but earth and ashes"[99]—there are times when one can, and indeed must, argue with God. Arguing with God has a strong tradition in Jewish culture[100] and it begins here, with Abraham.

Abraham is the first person in Scripture to be called a Prophet (Hebrew: *navi*) His role is two-fold. He defends humanity to an angry God, while acting as His representative, as when Abraham prays for the life of a local king, and to unblock the sealed wombs of the palace women. Abraham's most poignant role is as the original human rights activist, demanding that God Himself be subject to His own laws: "The judge of all the earth—will he not do what is just?"[101] No one, not even God, is above universal principles of justice and the rule of law.

When the bargaining had ended, Abraham felt he had saved the city of Sodom. On the following day, he saw the smoke rising from this holocaust like the "dense-smoke pouring out of a potter's kiln."[102] It is his confrontation with the collective Shadow, a necessary moment of disillusionment. Abraham, now, understood the reality of human evil. This moment is one of the great moments of silence in Scripture.

Abraham's striking ability to question injustice and speak his mind makes his silence at the injustice of the *akeda* all the more poignant. Abraham is a man who can and did question God. At *akeda*, he **chose** not to.

Given his experience of Sodom and of Ishmael, Abraham, I believe, understood the *akeda* was something he had to go through. Philosophers, from Immanuel Kant to Martin Buber challenged Abraham's readiness to accept the voice as divine: how did Abraham know that the voice was of God and not of the devil? Can one always distinguish Shadow from Self? Despite the overt immorality of the call, Abraham never doubted that it was from the Divine. Just as previously, he had said that God may not do what is unjust, I imagine Abraham could not imagine the Divine asking him to do something immoral.

The nature of *akeda* is elaborated by two Hebrew words, *hineini* and *yachdav*, which are each repeated three times during the short 19 lines of the *akeda* story. "*Hineni*" means "Here I am" and derives from the word for "here." When God first calls Abraham by name, "Abraham, Abraham," he replies, "*Hineini*," "Here I am." When Isaac calls him "Father" to ask his question, Abraham again answers "*Hineini*." The third and final "*hineini*" comes at the climactic moment when the angel-messenger calls Abraham to do no harm to his son. Abraham's word, "*Hineini*," "Here I am," or in a bolder translation, "Ready!" will become the standard to how a prophet responds to a Divine Call. When they are first called, Moses, Samuel, Isaiah, each says, *hineini*, "Ready!" *Hineini* indicates a readiness to hear and to be fully present. It indicates an existential attitude needed to be fully ready to listen to the Voice, to the Call, and to our patients: In the "here I am," I am intensely listening, ready to respond.

The other word, *yachdav*, means "together" and is derived from the word for "one" or "unity," *echad*. The word *echad* completes that most fundamental Hebrew prayer, the *sh'ma*, "Hear, O Israel, the Lord, Our God, the Lord is **One**."[103] *Yachdav* is a state of being united, all together. It appears three times in Genesis 22: First, when father and son leave their servants behind and go off on their mission *together*; again, after Abraham's wisely evasive reply to Isaac's question, "Here are the fire and the wood, but where is the lamb for the offering-up?" To which his father replies: "God will see for himself to the lamb for the offering-up, my son." The narrator adds: The two of them went **together**. Finally, when Abraham returns to his lads, but without Isaac, to go **together** back home to Beersheva.

Even though the *akeda* deals with a most brutal separation, the underlying leitmotif is a symphony of togetherness. Midrash traditionally explains that the second *"yachdav"* as representing Isaac's intuitive understanding that he is the one to be sacrificed. Like Jesus, Isaac accepts his fate and goes, together with his father toward it. Together these two words present the essence of Abraham's message to his son and in a way to us. The first is the need to be ready, ready to respond. The second is the fundamental importance of togetherness, unity and comm-unity; and the third is that within all of us is the need to be true to your Self. It is a high-wire act that we are all on.

Nevertheless, the question remains: Why does God need to test Abraham? Or rather, why have Abraham undergo a test? To understand the nature of the test, I must make a detour to the "psychology of revolutionary." Normally, family life is based on bio-logical continuity, the ongoing bond between parents and children, who in turn become parents. Revolutionaries, in contrast, reject biological kinship. Instead, they substitute a kinship of individuals totally identified with a common ideology and mission. Solidarity among comrades is intense; relatives and friends who do not share this ideological commitment become outsiders, even strangers. Revolution requires a dramatic break with the past in order to create a new heaven on earth. This was true of the Zionist Socialists who founded the egalitarian kibbutz in Israel, as well as the Bolsheviks who wished to take the people into the Promised Land of a classless society. Once successful, every revolutionary eventually faces the dilemma of continuity: how do I pass on the spirit of the revolution to the next generation? The revolutionary founder, whether spiritual or political, has a secret: the unacknowledged guilt of abandoning his Father; how can he be certain his own "sons" will not do the same? Paradoxically, how does a revolutionary assure his sons be loyal to a tradition of disloyalty?

Anthropologists divide succession into two main types: by birthright and by selection. The benefit of birthright is an assured, pre-determined tradition. Everyone knows who will be the next king, priest, or CEO. The downside is that new leader may be ill-prepared or catastrophically inadequate. Hereditary kingship, whether in ancient China, Egypt, or Rome, is proof of that fact. Succession by birthright involves trading off the benefits of security for the risks of incompetence.

Charismatic patterns of selection through ability is the mirror image of birthright. The new leader is dynamic and highly capable, but the transition may be uncertain, violent, even leading to civil war. Often, the best approach is to combine aspects of both systems. Moses, a returning political refugee rose to authority as a charismatic leader, but he passed on political leadership to his chosen successor, Joshua. In contrast, he created a hereditary priest-caste based in his own clan and family, beginning with his own brother, Aaron. Every Cohen, Kagan, or Katz is a priest-descendant of Moses' brother who still plays a significant role in Jewish ritual. Likewise, the high point of the Roman Empire occurred when a series of emperors adopted worthy successors as sons, combing a charismatic succession with a fictive kinship; when Marcus Aurelius named his own biological son as emperor, profound catastrophe immediately followed. In the Old Testament alone, there are 28 cases of father-to-son inheritance and in **none** is there a single, clear-cut case where a father simply and successfully initiates his firstborn son to be his chosen heir and spiritual successor. Biblical fathers, Adam, Jacob, Samuel, or David experienced traumatic losses of their sons. The *akeda* is, therefore, part of a pervasive pattern of traumatic succession.

Birthright succession need not be biological. In academics, researchers are evaluated by their "doctoral fathers" and not by their actual work. Succession in psychoanalytic institutes is often based upon who your analyst was rather than analytical achievement. Kirsner, who studied four American psychoanalytic institutes, found that often the analytic "fathers" manipulate those they train into carrying out their wishes, pressuring their followers to become apostles.[104] Freud set the tradition in this regard. Despite the persona of professional organization, he manipulated from behind the scenes via The Secret Committee. These compliant "sons" lived constricted, obedient lives, complying with old theories and methods, vying to be each more faithful and unoriginal than the next. Those who do break away and become independent are "destined to feel guilty for killing off their fathers." Revolutionaries, therefore, have intensely ambivalent relationships with their own children. They yearn for them to continue their revolution and fear them for their independence. This is exactly what happened when the Revolutionary Founder Freud fainted at the thought that his Crown Prince Jung had "death wishes" to him. Freud's fainting was related to his Laius complex. He experienced Jung as a displacing son. The double bind was that Freud wanted Jung to be loyal to him personally, and yet loyal to the revolutionary movement of psychoanalysis. It was a tension Freud was unable to hold. Jung was exiled and cast out as Lucifer. The secret committee that replaced Jung became followers who sacrificed their own creativity on the altar of loyalty. To put the conundrum of revolutionary succession in a different way: How can a revolutionary's own son become the revolutionary's disciple trusted to carry on the revolution? This is the heart of Abraham's crisis.

At the beginning of his spiritual journey, an unknown Voice sent Abraham off to an unknown place. Listening to the Voice meant leaving his past behind, breaking from his father-bound identity and literally abandoning his elderly father. The Hebrew phrase, *lech lecha* usually translated as "leave" or "go-you-forth" is literally, "Go to yourself," initiating Abraham on a journey toward a destiny and a destination of his own.

The search to become a father in his own right is the psychic energy that powers his life story. To discover his own God, however, he must leave his father's gods. This conflict is expressed in well-known Midrash,[105] a kind of Rabbinic active imagination, about Abraham's early life with father. According to that tradition, Abraham's father made and sold statutes of "gods" made of wood and stone. One day, the father left the young Abraham in charge of the store—a rite of passage. Abraham picked up his father's hammer and proceeded to smash all the gods, except the largest one in whose hand he placed the hammer. When his father returned, he saw the terrible damage and asked his son what had happened. Abraham calmly told his father that the "gods" started arguing among themselves as to who was more powerful. They started fighting and so destroyed each other until only the strongest one was left. His father said: "Don't you know they are only blocks of wood and stone?" Young Abraham replied with youthful *chutzpa*:

"If they are only wood and stone, why do you worship them?"

There are many readings of the legend but it clearly places the issue of continuity and disruption at the forefront. Abraham, the trickster rebel, does not directly confront his father. Nevertheless, he does subvert his fathers' gods, and destroys them and his father's god-image. Jung, no doubt, would approve that young Abraham was not striking out at his personal father from a regressive Oedipal complex, but only attacking his ideology, as Akhenaton did to his father.

Abraham's father, Terah, has another hidden, unconscious influence on Abraham and his new god-image. Abraham's first journey lay in the shadow of his father's previous trek from Ur, near Basra, in southern Iraq. When Abraham's father set out with his family from southern Iraq, his declared destination was Canaan. For some unstated reason, he stopped halfway across the Fertile Crescent, roughly in modern Kurdistan. Years later, Abraham set out on his own journey. Only when Abraham arrives in Canaan, does he learn that he has reached his destination. Abraham "unconsciously" completed his father's unfulfilled dream so that Abraham could now say, "Father, I have arrived, where you wanted to go." As Jung said: "Nothing has a stronger influence psychologically... on their children than the unlived life of the parent."[106] Abraham's developing "god-image" was emerging from his unconscious, father-bound imago. Abraham only becomes entirely free of his positive father

WHY ABRAHAM AGREED TO KILL

complex when his own name is changed from *Av-ram*, meaning, "father is supreme" to *Av-raham*, meaning "Father of Many Nations."[107] As Av-raham, the Hebrew for Abraham, he becomes a Great Father in his own right.

Now we are in a position to understand how *akeda* resolved the revolutionary's crisis of continuity by recreating for the son, the spiritual journey of the father. Even in translation, one can hear how poetic cadence of the *akeda* echoes the rhythm of his first call toward his destiny:

> "Leave your country, your family, your
> father's house,
> "Take your son, your only-one, whom
> you love, Yitzhak
> to the land I will let you see."[108]
> and go-you-forth to the land of Moriyya/
> Seeing."[109]

In both cases, Abraham is told to go to an unknown location. Setting out for the unknown is central to any spiritual quest or deep analysis—if you know where you are going, then you are probably not heading in the right direction; in taking Isaac and two lads, he is literally taking Isaac away from the world of women into the world of masculine. Their journey recreates Abraham's earlier journey throughout Canaan as a pilgrim to the Self. Later, father and son, separate from the lads in a further stage of individuation. Most

115

dramatically, Abraham recreates the situation in which he challenged Divine authority at Sodom—Isaac's question clearly shows he has learned the tradition of challenging authority. Abraham's creative response teaches him something profound about trusting the Process: "God will see for himself to the lamb for offering-up, my son."[110] But most of all, the *akeda* is how Abraham introduces Isaac to the divine, prophecy, promises, and the transcendent; Abraham gives Isaac away and gets him back. Then he leaves Isaac to work things out for himself alone—rather like the vision quest of Sioux Indians—or the long periods of intense solitude characteristic of the great philosophers. Isaac offered up as Abraham's son is reborn as prophet of Abraham's God. Choosing God, Abraham received God choosing his son as a man of God.

Freud claimed that there is no need in childhood as strong as the need for a father's protection.[111] This is very true, but so is the opposite. Fathers do need to know when it is time to allow their sons and daughters to explore on their own, unprotected. A father's belief that their offspring can do it on their own provides an enormous psychic protection. The next time, we meet Isaac, he is walking and meditating in the field. The *akeda* has clearly broken his maternal symbiosis and forced him to come to grips with his destiny and survivor mission. At the same time, he meets his future wife Rebecca, who comforts him from the death of his mother, and the Text adds "and he loved her."[112] It is the only time such a romantic phrase is found in all of Hebrew Scripture. For Isaac, this traumatic encounter with death made him into a survivor, much as Abraham had come away from the smoking furnace of Sodom with a sense of having been saved for some special purpose. The blessings addressed to Abraham were his first revelation to continue the spiritual revolution of his father. Isaac was indeed bound to the God of Abraham. The *akeda,* from this perspective was a creative trauma, a ritual ordeal and initiation into relationship with the Divine. Abraham had been forced to choose between his son and his Self/Destiny; Isaac now must discover what it means to be chosen.

Coda:

The *akeda* story embodies another archetypal experience beyond the realm of fathers and sons. It is an intrusion of the sacred into the everyday. It is the experience of losing something precious—your keys, your computer file, your child—being saturated with anxiety and despair and worse. And then. Suddenly. An epiphany. The keys, files, or child are found! It is a moment of miraculously inspired synchronicity. Life is hopeful, exuberant, you feel like hugging and singing. This is an experience that the *akeda* conveys to me most strongly: having lost all, you receive it back again. The next time, you find that lost object and rejoice, look up toward an unknown place and think of Abraham.

Why Did Lot's Wife Look Back?

Inspired by the strange salt sculptures standing at the southern end of the Dead Sea, Lot's wife looking back, is one of the most enduring images in the entire Bible. As she flees the desolating destruction of their city, the angel-messengers who have come to save them, warn her and her family not to look back. Their guardians instruct them: "Escape for your life, do not gaze behind you, do not stand still anywhere in the Plain."[113] But Lot's wife ignores their warning. She turns back and is transformed into a pillar of salt. Anyone who sees the strange pillars can well understand why they were associated with that story of divine disaster. What remains unclear is **why** Lot's wife deliberately decided to ignore the advice of her guides and bring her famous fate upon herself. Why did she look back?

There is another tragic story that shows how catastrophic looking back prematurely can be. It is the terrible tale from Greek mythology of a master musician, Orpheus and his beloved fiancé, Eurydice.[114] Orpheus's bride, bitten by a snake, dies on the way to their wedding ceremony and descends to the Underworld. Orpheus' mourning music makes even the gods weep. Through the magic of his music, Orpheus convinces the king and queen of the Underworld, Hades and Persephone, to allow him to bring his bride back into life. Persephone, herself, endlessly rotates between the lower and upper world, spending half the year with her husband and half the year with her mother. They permit Orpheus to do so on one condition. He must not look back to gaze upon Eurydice's face until she has reached the surface world. No reason is given. But it does have the feel of a test of moral endurance. Orpheus, serenades her almost to safety but true to traditions of Greek tragedy, makes a fateful decision that brings catastrophic consequences for him and his beloved. Just as they are about to reach the warmth of light, Orpheus looks back and loses his beloved forever. The myth does not specify why Orpheus looked back. Was it a searing separation anxiety that she was no longer behind him? Or, a sudden impulse to see her loving face? Perhaps, he was drawn to do the very thing that is most forbidden? Orpheus' motivation does not yield to any simple solution. But it does show how love's resurrection can be destroyed in a single, mistimed, backward glance.

Lot's wife and Orpheus do have some things in common. Their looking back occurs at a moment of intense psychological trauma and loss. Within the destruction of the cities of the Plain, Lot's family presents a psychological panorama of how people respond to trauma. The first and perhaps most common response to

120

an imminent threat of extreme disaster is denial: It cannot be true. When Lot tells his Sodom-dwelling sons-in-law of the impending catastrophe, they say, "Surely, you must be joking!" From holocaust to hurricane, people tend to disbelieve the clear and present evidence that grave danger is near at hand. They will seize upon any ambiguity to interpret the situation overly optimistically, until it is too late. Individuals with previous experience of disaster and so are "disaster-prepared," do best and are least vulnerable to its most toxic consequences. Surviving a previous event seems to inoculate a person from the worst long-term effects.

The accounts of impact of intense combat stress whether in civil war (called "irritable heart" by Da Costa, or "shell shocked" from the Great War) are strikingly similar to Vietnam Vets, for whom the term post-traumatic stress disorder (PTSD) was first coined.[115] These victims of trauma are psychologically consumed by traumatic experiences and it is in this context that we can understand the wisdom of the advice of the angel-messengers. In order to escape the very worst negative psychological effects, survivors need to create a psychic distance between themselves and the black hole of the trauma. Turning back prematurely is the symbolic equivalent of being swept into a vortex and not being able to get clear. Survivors may emerge physically intact but permanently disabled. They are unable to resume their previous identity and existence. Instead, their identity as a survivor overtakes them. They become emotionally frozen within the psychological confines of the event, often experienced in recurring nightmares, in which they relive the experience night after night. Traumatic events often leave victims permanently scarred, and there are clear reports that go back to antiquity. The famous English diarist Samuel Pepys survived the Great Fire of London in 1666, but later feared sleep because of recurring nightmares of the fire.[116]

Many of the characteristics of PTSD including flashbacks, dissociation or a disconnect from feelings, feeling numb, avoiding anything connected to trauma, losing interest in the world, yet being easily startled are all symbolized in the fate of Lot's wife, frozen in the fate of looking back at the trauma. Her image as a standing pillar of salt is an evocative image of a person frozen in PTSD.

If Lot's wife personifies the acute, frozen numbing PTSD response, then her husband Lot exemplifies a more insidious, chronic variant. He has come to Sodom as an economic migrant where he married and raised four daughters. When the messenger-angels arrive, Lot rises to greet them bowing low to the ground. Over their protests, he convinces them to come to his house for hospitality. Like Abraham, Lot is someone who knows how to honor guests. Just after they have eaten but before sleep, all the men of the town come to Lot's door and demand "to know" the strangers. "Know" in Biblical Hebrew often has a sexual meaning, as when "Adam knew his wife Eve." The Sodomites, true to their name, are planning a gang homosexual rape. In the Middle East, hospitality is a sacred trust and one defends one's guests with one's life. Lot, however, does not. Instead, Lot does something so strange that it defies paternal imagination. He offers his two younger, virgin daughters to be gang raped instead! His offer is bizarre, even by Biblical standards, and undoubtedly plays a role on how these daughters behave later in the story. What Lot's offer reveals is the profound patriarchy of his society. A father had absolute control of his daughters and their sexuality. Similarly, when Lot warns the rest of his family, he consults only with his sons-in-law and does not bother even to speak with his own married daughters. The messengers save Lot by striking the mob with dazzling light—a truly ironic image, given their moral blindness. They pull Lot inside to safety and shut the door. They warn Lot of the impending disaster. As the messengers urge him to escape into the safety of the hill country, Lot pleads weakness and is allowed to stop at a small town and then settles in a cave. Lot proceeds to become an alcoholic, recalling his ancestor, the first Biblical PTSD survivor, Noah. After surviving the Flood, Noah was the first person to plant vineyards, make wine and become an alcoholic. His nakedness is exposed by his youngest son, while he himself was in a drunken stupor.[117] Both PTSD and alcohol problems often occur together.[118] Between a quarter to three-quarters of survivors of abuse, or violent trauma, report problematic alcohol use. The majority of Vietnam veterans seeking treatment for

PTSD abuse alcohol. Alcoholism becomes a way of trying to forget, or rather to blot out the memory of what cannot be forgotten.

The last act in the Lot family drama is the most remarkable of all. Disasters rarely cause severe breakdowns of moral codes. More often catastrophe brings people together within a community feeling of solidarity of having gone through something special together. Lot's two youngest daughters display such "disaster solidarity." They believe that they are the sole survivors of the nuclear-like holocaust and feel that humankind itself is in danger of extinction. As a result, they make an audacious plan. They will make their father drink until he has passed out. Then each in turn will lie with him to "keep seed alive by our father." In terms of survivor psychology, these sisters formulate an outrageous survivor mission that defies a universal taboo. They work together, the elder leading and guiding her younger sister, who is nevertheless a full partner. The contrast with the better-known sisters, Rachel and Leah, who do experience bitter sexual competition and reproductive envy, is striking, even painful. Within the Biblical worldview, the contrast between these sisters-becoming-mothers and the product of their paternal incest is remarkable. Theses sisters were considered the founding matriarchs of the neighbors and traditional enemies of the Hebrew Nation, the Moabites and Ammonites, who lived in what is today the Hashemite Kingdom of Jordan. Their names are mockingly said to reflect their mythical, incestuous origin; for example, "Moab" is given a folk etymology of "from the father" (Hebrew, *me'av*).[119] Yet, these extraordinary sisters remain among the greatest heroines in all of Scripture, reflecting the idea that catastrophe sometimes brings out the best in us.

There is one more survivor who must be considered and he is Abraham. Abraham was warned in advance about the impending disaster. In his extraordinary debate with the Divine Presence, he argued that there must be at least 50, 45, 30, 20, at least 10 just, good men for whom the city must be saved. When the dialogue had ceased, Abraham must have thought that he has convinced Him to stop for the sake of those ten good and just men. But, the next day, when Abraham awoke, he looked down and saw dense-smoke going up like dense-smoke billowing out of a potter's kiln. In sharp contrast to Lot's wife who was psychically "too close," for example, to the trauma, Abraham saw what happened with true psychic perspective.

On the one hand, Abraham must have felt a deep feeling of failure that he failed to prevent the catastrophe. Abraham must have understood how naïve he had been concerning the pervasiveness of human evil in the city. He learned the bitter principle that evil flourishes when good men step aside. On the other hand, seeing terrifying power of Divine vengeance, made Abraham into a survivor who has survived for a reason and so carries the intense imprint of a survivor mission. The survivor mission is passed on from generation to generation.

Abraham is charged to teach his children, his children's children and ever after, the ethical imperative: "to do what is right and just."[120] His descendants, in turn, inherit this survivor mission. If they abandon the moral imperative of their Great Ancestor, they too may suffer the annihilating fate of Sodom. Throughout the Bible, Sodom remains an image of ultimate horror, "a desolation forever," for those who do evil and abandon the Way.[121]

Nevertheless, the question remains: why did Lot's wife turn back, when her husband and daughters did not. Lot, as the Sodomites repeatedly emphasize is a newcomer, a resident alien, "one who came to sojourn and wants to play the judge."[122] He has never been accepted as "one of us." With Abraham, he has traveled the entire course of the Fertile Crescent. Lot is a man who knows how to reestablish his home again and again. But for his wife, Sodom was the only home she has known. Leaving home is rarely simple, even when it is a normal developmental process of separating from parental nest, as when one goes off to college or the Army. Yet, for Lot's wife, it is an unwanted separation from origin, identity, and security. Becoming a refugee inevitably involves an ambivalent process of mourning. Mourning, first, involves accepting the reality of the loss. Eventually, emotional energy lodged in the dead can be gradually withdrawn, reabsorbed and reinvested in some new object. A spouse dies; at first, one feels lost, aimless, yearning; life seems pointless without them. Freud wisely understood that a person in the acme of grief resembles patients who are depressed. Gradually, the psyche begins to accept the new reality and the psyche becomes reinvigorated with renewed eros and energy. Eventually, new loving may become possible. Likewise, the exile needs to separate from one's home country emotionally in order be able to invest in his new host country. Exiles and refugees remain with a divided loyalty between home country and their adopted one. They must find a way to live with the tension between the two. The danger is that one may be stuck, "fixated" in stage of nostalgia and not have any free energy to invest in the current reality. I believe that was the case for Lot's wife. She could not emotionally detach from her hometown and contemplate a life outside it. This is the metaphorical existence of migrants, exiles and refugees who live physically in their host country but who are essentially pining for their (now idealized) native land. Like Lot's wife, they are frozen within the emotional orbit of a lost home, unable to separate and unable to reattach.

Finally, Lot's actions show the depth of the patriarchal society in which he lived. The actions of Lot's wife, as well as his daughters provide a severe critique of that worldview. Lot's wife refuses to listen to the advice of the messengers and her husband. Defying these sensible male figures, she would rather die than leave. His daughters clearly feel that their father's offering them for gang rape liberates them from any fatherly control. As a result, they are free to make their own sexual choices and determine their own sexual destiny, as women liberated from Father. Freudians may see in their actions a secret wish for their father and a father's unconscious erotic desire to make love with their daughters, but this is to miss the point. Their determination to reproduce is exactly what Lot's wife lacked. These two sisters were willing to do whatever it took, in order to make a new start. They show how survivors, exiles, even refugees may live out the archetypal drama of death and rebirth.

Notes

[1] Rainer, M. R. (1993). 6ᵗʰ Letter. In *Letters to a Young Poet* (pp. 52-3). M. D. Herder (Trans.). NY: Norton.

[2] The Bhagavada Gita forms a part of the *Mahabharata*, but is often published as a separate text. Many translations exist. I have relied upon a reprint of a 19ᵗʰ century Victorian translation: *Bhagavada Gita* (1993) Sir E. Arnold (Trans.). NY: Dover Publications.

[3] Mahabharata is a living oral epic and its telling is a unique form of "performance art" in many Indian languages. Nevertheless, many translations, both scholarly and popular, do exist. Some popular, highly edited versions include: John-Claude Carriere. (1988). *The Mahabharata: A Play based upon the Indian Epic*. London: Metheun, which formed the basis of Peter Brook's stage version and epic film, available on video. For a scholarly version, see the multi-volume but uncompleted version by J.A.van Buitenen, now being continued by James Fitzgerald. (1992). *The Mahabharata*. IL: University of Chicago Press. Quotes used come from P. Lal, *The Mahabharata of Vyasa*. New Delhi: Vikas Publishing.

[4] Dunn, J., and P. Munn (1987). Development of justifications in disputes with mother and child. *Developmental Psychology* 23:791-98.

[5] The first account of successful transgender surgery involved a Danish painter Einar Wegener who became Lili Elbe in 1930. However, the best-known case involved Christine Jorgensen, an American GI who had a sex-change operation, also in Denmark. Since then tens of thousands of individuals, suffering from "gender dysphoria" have undergone sex-reassignment surgery and many more use hormones, without altering their genital structure. A good introduction to the topic is, Randi Ettner, Gender Loving Care: A Guide to Counseling Gender-Variant Clients.
The first and still classic text is Harry Benjamin. (1966). *The Transsexual Phenomenon*, which is available free online at http://www.symposium.com along with other historical papers. The appendix of Benjamin's book, written by Richard Green, Transsexualism: Mythological, historical and cross-cultural aspects, summarizes historical and ethnological material.

[6] Deuteronomy 22:5

[7] The best studies of Hijra are: Nanda, S. (1998). *Neither Man Nor Woman: The Hijras of India*. Belmont, CA: Wadsworth Publishing; and Reddy, G. (2005). *With Respect to Sex: Negotiating Hijra Identity in South India*. IL: University of Chicago.

[8] For more on Mahu, see Matzner, A. (2001). *'O Au No Keia: Voices from Hawai'i's Mahu and Transgender Communities*. Bloomington, Indiana: Xlibris.

[9] The best-known sequential hermaphrodite fish is the sea bass; there are 21 families of hermaphrodite fish.

[10] For more on Daniel Screiber and his father, see Schatzman, M. (1973). *Soul Murder: Persecution in the Family*. London: Allen Lane.

[11] Levine, S. B. & Davis, L. (2002). What I did for Love: temporary returns to the male gender role. *The International Journal of Transgenderism, 6*, (4). It is available at http://symposium.com/ijt.

[12] The quote is from the opening scene of the movie, "Patton."

[13] The "winning" quote is often attributed to Vince Lombardi, the legendary coach of the Green Bay Packers, for whom the Super Bowl trophy is named, but it was first stated by UCLA American football coach, "Red" Saunders. (Wikipedia)

[14] I have relied on *Homer, The Odyssey*. (1937). W.H.D. Rouse (Trans.). London: Thomas Nelson.

[15] Leader, C. (2009). The Odyssey – a Jungian perspective: Individuation and meeting with the archetypes of the collective unconscious. *British Journal of Psychotherapy* 25(4):506 –519; Russo, J. (2008). *A Jungian analysis of Homer's Odyssey,* Cambridge Companion to Jung. P. Young-Eisendrath & T. Dawson (Eds.). (pp. 253-268). Cambridge University Press.

[16] Li Po and Tu Fu. *Poems*. (1973). A. Cooper (Ed. & Trans.). Translator notes: "This must be the best known now of all Chinese poems, especially among overseas Chinese." p. 109. Harmondsworth, UK: Penguin Books.

[17] Basho, M. (1966). *The Narrow Road to the Deep North*. Harmondsworth: Penguin.

[18] Jung, C. G. (1963). The Tower. In *Dreams Memories, Reflections* (Chap. 8, p. 252). London & Glasgow: Collins.

[19] Frost, R. (1962). The Death of a Hired Hand. In *A Concise Treasury of Great Poems*. L. Untermeyer (Ed.) (pp. 434-5). New York: Perma Books.

[20] Abramovitch, H. (1975). Tromba: A Spirit Possession cult in ile Sainte-Marie de Madagascar. *Taloha, Winter*; and (2000). Good Death and Bad Death: Therapeutic Implications of Cultural Conceptions of Death and Bereavement. In R. Malkinson, S. S. Rubin, & E. Witztum (Eds.), *Traumatic and Nontraumatic Loss and Bereavement* (Chap. 10, pp. 255-272). Madison, CT.: Psychosocial Press.

[21] Schutz, A. (1945). The Homecomer. *American Journal of Sociology* 50 (5):369-376. A seminal article on dilemmas faced by those who return home based on research on returning American soldiers. Thanks to Edna Lomsky-Feder for pointing it out to me.

[22] Babylonian Talmud, Ta'anit 23a.

[23] Cooper Marcus, C. (2006). *House as a Mirror of Self: Exploring the Deeper Meaning of Home,* 2nd revised edition (p. xvi). York Beach, Maine: Nicholas-Hays.

[24] Zemon Davis, N. (1984). *The Return of Martin Guerre.* The actual case is much more complicated than the movie. Cambridge, MA: Harvard University Press.

[25] Plato. *Phaedo.* B. Jowett (Trans.). Available in The Gutenberg Book Project: https://www.gutenberg.org/files/1658/1658-h/1658-h.htm

[26] One scholar lists 21 distinct interpretations of the last words: 1. Socrates is raving deliriously. 2. Socrates is asking Asclepius to return Socrates from the dead. 3. Socrates is being deliberately enigmatic. 4. Socrates is offering a gift to avert misfortune after death. 5. Socrates dies conscious of his own immortality andtherefore sacrifices to Asclepius, who could raise the dead. 6. Socrates is grateful for cure from doubts about the soul's immortality; Socrates had become doubtful as one after another argument for immortality appeared flawed; his concluding myth removed Socrates' uncertainty. 7. Socrates is thanking Asclepius for having been cured of life, which Socrates views as a disease. 8. Socrates is bribing Asclepius to avert death. 9. Socrates is petitioning Asclepius to release himself and his friends from the Orphic cycle of reincarnation. 10. Socrates is asking his friends to commemorate his death with a ritual meal of the sacrificed rooster. 11. Socrates is remembering a past unpaid debt to Asclepius. 12. Socrates is thanking Asclepius for healing Plato from serious illness that kept Plato away from Socrates' final hours: a dying prophetic vision tells Socrates that Plato is healed. 13. Socrates is showing gratitude to Asclepius for Plato, whose writings would be a remedy for Socrates' being forgotten. 14. Socrates is jokingly thanking Asclepius, by offering the rooster, a conventional gift to a homosexual lover, because Socrates is having an erection as he dies; the erection naturally accompanies the process of dying but also results from the touching of Socrates' genital area by the poison bearer as he confirmed that Socrates' body was becoming cold. 15. Socrates thanks Asclepius, who presides over drugs, for a painless death. 16. Speaking not as patient, but as healer of the soul with Socratic discussion, Socrates thanks Apollo, patron of healers, through Asclepius, Apollo's son. 17. Socrates thanks Asclepius for Crito's cure from the malaise of attraction to certain bad arguments; these were arguments that Socrates should escape from prison that Crito gave in the dialogue, arguments from which Socrates dissuaded Crito. 18. The cock to Asclepius replaces the libation Socrates was not allowed to pour from the hemlock; libation was not allowed because the drink was exactly measured to effect execution. 19. Socrates thanks Asclepius for having cured Socrates' friends in the Phaedo discussion from the malady of mistrust of argument; that malady threatened when arguments for immortality

that at first were appealing were shown faulty. 20. Socrates thanks Asclepius because Socrates dies morally healthy, with no vices. 21. Socrates thanks Asclepius for good care throughout life.

[27] Nietzsche in *The Gay Science*, 340.

[28] The text of Socrates' reply to Crito is: "Nothing particular, Crito," he replied. "Only, as I have always told you, take care of yourselves; that is a service which you may be ever rendering to me and mine and to all of us, whether you promise to do so or not. But if you have no thought for yourselves, and care not to walk according to the rule which I have prescribed for you, not now for the first time, however much you may profess or promise at the moment, it will be of no avail."

[29] Rav Hisda, Talmud Bavli, Brachot, 55a.

[30] Xenophon. *The Memorabilia* (IV,7,9).

[31] The one delivered from illness or danger says in Hebrew: "Blessed are You, LORD our God, King of the Universe, Who bestows good things upon the unworthy, and has bestowed upon me every goodness." The congregation responds: "Amen. He Who has bestowed upon you every goodness, may He [continue to] bestow upon you every goodness. Selah."

[32] Talmud Brachot 54b: "Rav Yehuda said in the name of Rav, four kinds of people must recite the Birkat HaGomel (Blessing for Deliverance): Those travelling by sea upon docking, those travelling through the desert upon reaching an inhabited settlement, one who was ill and recovered, and one who was incarcerated and then freed."

[33] Donne, J. Holy Sonnets: Death, be not proud. https://www.poetryfoundation.org/poems/44107/holy-sonnets-death-be-not-proud

[34] Coelho, P. (2007). *Veronika Decides to Die.* (pp. 87-8) Quote by Dr. Igor. New York, et. al.: Harper Perennial.

[35] Šakić, V., Franc, R., Ivičić, I., & Maričić, J. (2007). Tie – an Accessory Fashion Detail or a Symbol? *Croatian Medical Journal, August,* 48(4): 419–430.

[36] zazzle.com

[37] Barrie, J. M. (1988 [1911]). *Peter Pan*, p. 22. London: Puffin.

[38] All quotes from: http://www.brainyquote.com/quotes/keywords/tie_3.html#QXwo6o5wk6EjzjIg.99

[39] Ryle, G. (1986 [1949]). *The Concept of Mind* (p. 313). Harmondsworth, UK: Penguin Books.

[40] Monk, Ray. (1990). *Ludwig Wittgenstein: The Duty of Genius* (the best biography of Wittgenstein). London: Jonathan Cape.

[41] Wittgenstein, Ludwig. (1961). *Tractatus Logico-Philosophicus*. D.F. Pears & B.F. McGuiness (Trans.). London: RKP.

[42] All quotes are found at: http://www.goodreads.com/quotes/tag/silence

[43] Masters, E. L. (1919). in L. Untermeyer (Ed.) *Modern American Poetry*. Silence (Poem 43). New York: Hartcourt, Brace & Company. Available via

Gutenberg Book Project: http://www.gutenberg.org/files/58992/58992-h/58992-h.htm

[44] Lebra, T.S. (2009). The cultural significance of silence in Japanese communication. *Multilingua* 6(4): 11-30.

[45] Grosz, S. (2013). *The Examined Life* (p. 5) for a poignant example. London: Chatto & Windus.

[46] http://www.goodreads.com/quotes/tag/silence

[47] Buber, M. (1973). *Meetings: Autobiographical Fragments.* (Chap. 15, A Conversation, pp. 45-6). M. Friedman (Ed. with introduction and bibliography). LaSalle, Illinois: Open Court Publishing.

[48] Balint, M. (1955). *The Doctor, his Patient and the Illness* (p. 239). London: Pitman Medical Publisher.

[49] Olinick, S. L. (1982). Meaning beyond words: Psychoanalytic perceptions of silence and communication, happiness, sexual love and death. *International Review of Psycho-Analysis 9(4)*, 461-70.

[50] Bhagavad Gita. 5:10

[51] A. Ronneberg & K. Martin (Eds.). (2010). *The Book of Symbols.* Lotus (pp. 150-2). Cologne, Germany: Taschen.

[52] Jeremiah 1:6.

[53] Jonah 2:3. New Jerusalem Bible. Available, http://www.bibliacatolica.com.br/new-jerusalem-bible/jonah/2/#ixzz2b0HFYyYE

[54] Jonah 3:8-9.

[55] Jonah 4:2-3.

[56] Jonah 4:9.

[57] Jonah 4:10.

[58] Job 42: 2-6.

[59] Heschel, A. J. (1997). *God in Search of Man: A Philosophy of Judaism.* New York: Farrar, Straus & Giroux.

[60] Heller, J. (1984). *God Knows* (pp. 288-89). New York: Alfred A. Knopf.

[61] Mark 11:14.

[62] Matthew 21:8-22.

[63] "When a tree that bears fruit is cut down, its moan goes from one end of the world to the other, yet no sound is heard." (Pirket de-R. Eliezar, 34).

[64] Matthew 10:34-6.

[65] D. W. Winnicott. (1969). The Use of an Object. *International Journal of Psycho-Analysis,* 50:711-16.

[66] Jung, C. G. 7, para.78.

[67] A shorter version is recorded in Matthew: Jesus replied, "Truly I tell you, if you have faith and do not doubt, not only can you do what was done to the fig tree, but also you can say to this mountain, 'Go, throw yourself into the sea,' and it will be done. If you believe, you will receive whatever you ask for in prayer." (Matthew 21:21-2). Gospel quotes are from New Jerusalem Bible.

[68] Mark 11:22-25.

[69] All quotes about the Impossible are from: http://www.brainyquote.com/quotes/keywords/impossible.html

[70] Albert Camus, Caligula, Act 1, available online: http://faculty.cbu.ca/philosophy/caligula/act%20one.htm

[71] Micah 4:4, echoing Deuteronomy 8:7.

[72] Jeremiah 8:13.

[73] Matthew 25:29.

[74] Niddah 47a.

[75] "And they sewed the leaves of the fig [te'enah] together." R. Simeon b. Yohai said; "That is the leaf which brought the occasion [to'anah] – for death – into the world." (Genesis Rabbah 19:6c). See also Rashi.

[76] Mark 11:25.

[77] Abramovitch, H. (2014). *Brothers and Sisters: Myth and Reality.* Section based, in part, on my book. College Park: Texas A & M University Press.

[78] Job 1:5-6, JPS.

[79] Job 42:11, JPS.

[80] Job 42:11.

[81] Job 42:15, JB.

[82] Genesis 50:15-21.

[83] Job 42: 12, JPS.

[84] Abramovitch, H. (2010). *The First Father, Abraham: Psychology and Culture of a Spiritual Revolutionary.* 2nd edition. Parts of this chapter are based upon my book. Libertary.com.

[85] Genesis 22:1-19.

[86] Qu'ran does not specify the name of the sacrificed son. Sura (37:100-110) says only: "...he said: "O my son! I see in a vision that I offer thee in sacrifice: now see what is thy view!" (The son) said: "O my father! do as thou art commanded: thou will find me if Allah so wills, one practicing Patience and Constancy!" So when they had both submitted their wills (to Allah) and He had laid Him prostrate on his forehead (for sacrifice). We called out to him "O Abraham! Thou hast already fulfilled the vision!" But the majority of Islamic traditions identify him as Ishmael who is a willing victim.

[87] Abraham is known as "Abram" ("My Father is Great") until his dramatic name change to "Abraham" ("Father of Many Nations") at age 99 in Genesis 17:5; but for simplicity sake I refer to him as "Abraham" throughout the chapter.

[88] Lyrics available at bobdylan.com. Dylan's father was named Abraham. Highway 61 ran from Duluth, where he was born, to New Orleans.

[89] Matthew 27:46; Mark 15:34, quoting Psalm 22:1.

[90] Genesis 24:67. This is one of the very few passages in which it is stated that a man loves his wife.

[91] Matthew 2:16-8.

[92] Levinson, D. J. (1978). *The Seasons of a Man's Life*. New York: Knopf.
[93] Miller, A. (1990). *The Untouched Key: Tracing Childhood Trauma in Creativity and Destructiveness*. London: Virago. In their first encounter, God tells Abraham: "Terah took Abram his son…they set out together…to go to the land of Canaan. But when they came as far as Harran, they settled there." (11:31).
[96] Whiting, J.W.M., Kluckholhn, R. & Anthony, A. (1966). The function of male initiation ceremonies at puberty. *Psychoanalysis and Male Sexuality*, 39-55. H.M. Ruitenbeek (Ed.).
[98] E. Fox (Trans.). (1995). *The Five Books of Moses: A New Translation*. Genesis 18:23-25. New York: Schocken Books.
[100] Laytner, A. (1977). *Arguing with God: A Jewish Tradition*. Jason Aronson.
[102] Author's translation.
[103] Deuteronomy 6:4. The Shema is recited in daily prayers and are the traditional dying words of a Jew.
[104] Eisold, K. (1994). The intolerance of diversity in psychoanalytic institutes. *International Journal of Psycho-Analysis 75*, 785-800; Eisold, K. (2001). Institutional conflicts in Jungian analysis. *Journal of Analytical Psychology 46*, 335-354. Kirsch, Tom (2000). *The Jungians*. London: Routledge; Kirsner, Douglas (2000). *Unfree Association: Inside Psychoanalytic Institutes*. London: Process Press.
[105] Bereshit Rabbah 38:13; similar stories are told in Jubilees 12 and Qur'an 21:51-70.
[106] Jung, C. G. 4: 301-323.
[111] Freud, S. (1961 [1930]). *Civilization and its Discontents*. In J. Strachey (Ed. & Trans.), *The Standard Edition of the Complete Psychological Works of Sigmund Freud* (Vol. 21, pp. 57-145). London: Hogarth Press. (Original published 1930).
[114] See Ovid, *Metamorphoses* X, 1-105; XI, 1-66. A good, recent translation is: *The Metamorphoses of Ovid*. (1995). A. Mandelbaum (Trans.). New York: Harcourt Brace.

[115] Andreasen, N. C. (2010). Posttraumatic Stress Disorder: A History and a Critique. *Annals of the New York Academy of Sciences, October.*
[116] Entry for Thursday 28 February 1667.
[117] Genesis 9:20-26. Also, see my book, (2014) *Brothers and Sisters: Myth and Reality* (pp. 54-7) for discussion of this episode and other sibling stories in the Bible, College Station: University of Texas A & M University Press.
[118] Kofoed, L., Friedman, M.J., & Peck, R. (1993). Alcoholism and drug abuse in patients with PTSD. *Psychiatric Quarterly, Summer* 64(2), 151-171. See website of National Center for PTSD, http://www.ptsd.va.gov/index.asp.
[119] Genesis 19:37-38.
[120] Genesis 18:19.
[121] See Deuteronomy 29:21-5; Isaiah 1:9-10, 13:19-20; Jeremiah 23:14, 49:18, 50:40; Amos 4:11; and Zephaniah 2:9.
[122] Genesis 19:9.